Fishing

FISHING

The Complete Guide to Basics

Craig Ritchie

KEY PORTER BOOKS

National Library of Canada Cataloguing in Publication Data

Ritchie, Craig
  Fishing : the complete guide to basics / Craig Ritchie ; foreword by Bob Izumi.

ISBN 1-55263-523-6

  1. Fishing—North America. 2. Freshwater fishes—North America.
I. Title.

SH462.R58 2003   799.1'1'097   C2002-906085-0

The publisher gratefully acknowledges the support of the Canada Council for the Arts and the Ontario Arts Council for its publishing program.

We acknowledge the financial support of the Government of Canada through the Book Publishing Industry Development Program (BPIDP) for our publishing activities.

Key Porter Books Limited
Six Adelaide Street East, Tenth Floor
Toronto, Ontario
Canada M5C 1H6

www.keyporter.com

Electronic formatting: Jean Lightfoot Peters

Printed and bound in Hong Kong, China

06 07 08 09 10 11 6 5 4 3 2 1

Contents

Getting Started

Bob Izumi

As the host of a nationally televised fishing show for more than eighteen years, I've had the opportunity to meet and talk fishing with thousands of anglers from all across North America, and it's amazing how many of these folks have only recently discovered fishing as a pastime. It seems that no matter where I travel, whether it's to shoot segments for the *Real Fishing Show*, to compete in a major tournament, or just to fish for fun, I meet people from all walks of life who share a great interest in fishing but also admit to feeling just a bit confused by it all—especially if they're new to the sport. While there are countless television fishing shows, fishing magazines, and fishing-related Web sites, most cater to anglers who already have some advanced level of fishing knowledge. There really isn't much out there for someone who's just starting out.

I've met people at remote fly-in fishing lodges in the Canadian Arctic who had spent thousands of dollars on equipment and travel to visit such remote destinations, but who simply didn't know how to cast or how to put line on their reel properly. Although these anglers were obviously very passionate about their fishing, there's no doubt that they would enjoy themselves even more if they had a better understanding of the basics. I'm always surprised at the number of letters I receive from viewers, and the number of people who write to our Web site, looking for basic fishing information: How do I select a rod and reel? What lures work best for different conditions? How do I find the fish in my favorite lake? What's the best time to go fishing? These are all very good questions, yet the answers aren't so easy to come by. This book attempts to change all that.

Craig Ritchie, who is himself an accomplished angler as well as a veteran outdoor writer, offers a comprehensive look at the world of freshwater fishing, starting with an up-close examination of the fish themselves. After all, the first step to catching fish is to learn a bit about them. So, logically, this book begins with a review of the major sporting species in North America.

You'll learn about the fish, and how fish relate to their environment, which will allow you to pinpoint productive fishing spots like a pro. Have you ever stood on the dock and looked out at a new lake, wondering where the fish are? By understanding how fish respond to wind, current, and water temperature, you'll be able to go to any body of water on the continent and, within a fairly short time, find all the most productive spots. Although there is always some element of luck in fishing, by knowing a bit about the fish and being able to find the places where they live, you stack the odds in your favor by a wide margin.

You'll then read about different lures and baits, rods and reels, and find out how the gear all works together. As a full-time fishing writer for the better part of two decades, Craig has enjoyed the opportunity to interview—and fish with—some of the best anglers in North America, and he passes along much of this wealth of experience. From assembling a basic lure kit to selecting live baits to matching rods and reels, you'll benefit from expert advice. And all the way through, Craig makes it interesting.

This was something I learned about him soon after we first met, a dozen years ago. We were videotaping a trout-fishing segment for the *Real Fishing Show* on a beautiful wooded creek in southern Ontario. We were fishing a small but deep pool that was absolutely rimmed with logs when Craig hooked a good rainbow of about six pounds (2.7 kg). As the silvery fish jumped all over the pool, Craig announced he had hooked several such fish from that spot but, due to the logs, had never landed any of them. I wanted him to catch the fish for the show, so I thought I should give him a hand landing it.

We were fishing from a high dirt bank that stood about four feet (1.2 m) above the water surface. I propped my rod against a nearby tree, then carefully picked my way down the steep bank and slid into the water, which was about thigh-deep. Craig worked the fish close, and after a few more moments I was able to grab it by the tail. With one hand around its tail and the other cradling it from beneath, it wasn't going anywhere.

With me in the water and Craig standing four feet above me, I knew it would make a difficult shot for the camera crew, so I casually said, "Hey Craig, come on down here and take a look at this fish," or something like that. I don't know if he slipped or the stream bank gave way, but a second later there was this huge splash as Craig fell off the bank and did a face-plant right into the river, almost drowning the $6,000 wireless microphone in the process.

Like I said, he always makes things interesting. Although I notice he didn't include a chapter about high-diving technique, this book does cover pretty much everything else.

One of the things I like best about fishing is that it's an evolutionary pastime. Things always change, so you never stop learning. Starting off with a solid understanding of the basics, however, makes the whole process easier. Because you'll be more successful, you'll have more fun. And isn't that the point of going fishing in the first place?

Acknowledgments

No one writes a book like this without help, and I'm no different. I would be remiss if I did not admit to owing a huge debt of gratitude to Bob Jones, Burt Myers, and Peter E. Sticklee, who pushed me along and encouraged me to pursue a career as a writer; the late Teddi Brown, who taught me the difference between quality writing and schlock; Frank Cicinelli, Joe Cutajar, Greg Elaschuk, John Hagerman, Mark Kulik, James Mouryas, and Dan Ralph, for years of friendship and making my time on the water so much more enjoyable; Bob Izumi, for selflessly teaching me so much about fishing; and my father, the late James Gordon Ritchie, who first talked me into impaling a worm on a hook.

So What Is It About Fishing, Anyway?

Fishing has captured our hearts and minds since we lived in caves. The discovery in Europe of ancient fish hooks fashioned from shattered bone proves that human beings fished with hook and line thousands of years ago, while half of the North American continent was still buried under several hundred feet of Wisconsonian glacier.

The basics of fishing haven't changed a great deal since that time. True, new materials and manufacturing technologies have allowed us to refine our equipment and make the whole thing easier. But the basics of outsmarting a fish remain pretty much the same. One of the earliest books on recreational fishing, Dame Juliana Berners' *Treatise on Fishing with an Angle*, published in the early sixteenth century, describes fly fishing for trout using techniques and strategies that are still practiced today. If nothing else, the lure of fishing has stood the test of time.

Government surveys reveal fishing to be one of the most popular recreational activities in North America, second only to swimming. In terms of participation, fishing is more popular than football, baseball, birdwatching, and golf *combined*. One in four adults owns a fishing license. In Canada alone, anglers spend in excess of $8 *billion* a year pursuing their favorite pastime. Spending in the United States is almost ten times that amount. Even in the downtown core of big cities across North America it's possible to find tackle shops tucked in between the bond brokers and the high-fashion boutiques. Take a drive in the country and it seems that every gas station and general store sells worms. Looks like that Huck Finn kid really was on to something after all.

So just what is it about fishing that makes it so popular? Fishing appeals to people for many reasons, some of them apparently contradictory. Some people fish to relax, while others say they crave the exhilaration. Still others cite the challenge of trying something new. There's the opportunity to enjoy the outdoors and escape the incessant din of telephones and daily life; the chance to spend quality time with family in beautiful surroundings; the opportunity to talk with your kids and not have to raise your voice to be heard over the Nintendo system. Fishing gives people—regardless of age, sex, or position in life—a chance to focus on a single goal for a period of time, putting aside thoughts of bills and retirement savings plans and mortgages and car payments and all those other things that tend to take up far too much of our attention.

Fishing can be as simple or as challenging as you care to make it. It can, and usually does, become a life-long pursuit, because you never stop learning about it. You can't outgrow it; just when you begin to think you know all there is to know, along comes some new twist to keep things interesting.

I think I was about seven years old when it all started for me. My family was vacationing at a rented cottage on a small lake in central Ontario's Haliburton Highlands. While Dad went about incinerating our dinner on the barbecue, I sat on the end of the dock with a stubby, solid fiberglass fishing rod and a small tub of worms, intent on resuming an ongoing tug-of-war with the perch and sunfish that lived under the wharf.

The dock itself was an ancient wooden affair that sat low on the water atop a series of broad wooden pilings that looked somewhat like chopped-off electricity poles. Over the three previous days I had learned that lowering my worm-baited hook along the shady side of the pilings would almost always result in an immediate bite, as one of the eager panfish gobbled up my bait. I would then unceremoniously lift the writhing fish from the water and admire it before slipping the coarse hook from its lip and releasing it to play again.

But one time it didn't happen quite that way. My rod tip bounced once, indicating that something was chewing away on the business end of my line, and I lifted on it as I had before. But instead of the happy tap-tap-tap I had grown to expect, I felt a heavy pull, followed by rapid, violent throbbing. Before I could utter a sound, this mammoth green fish—easily the size of our family cat—erupted from the water right beside the dock, twisting and gyrating furiously on the surface, its gill openings flared widely, mouth fully agape. Then, as quickly as it had appeared, it vanished again beneath the dock, leaving me thoroughly soaked, with a limp line and a bent hook. Dad, who had seen the fish jump, ran down to help, but by the time he reached the dock the behemoth—which I later learned was a largemouth bass—was gone.

Though I lost the fish, that instant of utter pandemonium changed me forever. For the rest of the week I continued to catch perch and sunfish, but it wasn't like before. Now my thoughts were solely on the big green bass. I wanted that fish—badly. I was now not just a fisherman, but a bass fisherman. A largemouth-bass specialist.

For the next two years I learned everything I could about largemouth bass. I collected pictures of them, which I taped to the walls in my bedroom. I read magazine articles and fishing books about them, and requested memberships in bass-fishing clubs for Christmas and birthday gifts. I watched who knows how many hours of television fishing shows about bass and no doubt drove everyone in my family out of their minds with my obsession. I was hooked.

Although I had more book smarts than practical experience, I nonetheless became a pretty reasonable bass fisherman. Subsequent cottage trips allowed me the opportunity to pursue the fish of my dreams. I even caught a few of them, something I now attribute as much to good luck as good planning. I was happily bewitched by bass until one cool Sunday afternoon in mid-October when my father took me for a drive. Our destination, only a few minutes away from our Toronto home, turned out to be across the road from the Humber River. While I waited for Dad, I wandered over to the riverbank. There, across the street from The Old Mill restaurant, sat a small flood control dam.

Upon reaching the water's edge, my jaw dropped slack and my eyes just about shot out of their sockets. To my utter disbelief, dozens of enormous red-and-black fish were leaping into the air, all across the face of the little dam. From pictures I had seen in fishing magazines I recognized the fish as coho salmon. I had read in one of my fishing magazines that Ontario had stocked some in the nearby Credit River the previous spring. These fish had evidently strayed east and wandered up the Humber by mistake.

In a nanosecond I shifted the focus of my life from bass fisherman to salmon angler. The bass were fun to catch—but these salmon were massive! Even the smallest of them could easily have eaten any of the bass I'd ever caught. And more importantly, they were a lot closer to home. To my delight I discovered that the Toronto subway crosses over the river, and there was a station just a few blocks away.

And so I became a diehard salmon angler. Being way too young to drive didn't matter. I would rise long before dawn and catch the first city bus of the day at 5:05 a.m. A short subway ride later, I arrived at the river. I would pull on waders and assemble my gear as the sun cracked a thin pink line in the eastern sky, fish straight through till dusk, then eat a chocolate bar for supper on the bus ride home. I would spend the evening patching leaky waders, sorting tackle, and planning strategy till finally succumbing to sleep somewhere around midnight. Five hours later I was up to do it all over again. That became my weekend routine through most of my teenage years.

While fishing on the river, I met some other kids of about the same age and we became good friends. We began taking pictures of each other with our big catches, and tied up our families' phone lines for hours through the week as we discussed the effects of recent weather systems, debated the merits of the new tackle we had bought or were planning to buy, and plotted where and how we would conquer the salmon on the upcoming weekend.

It's now a couple of decades later and I have to confess, things haven't changed much. I'm still learning about largemouth bass. And salmon too. And smallmouth bass. And pike. And muskie. And trout. My phone bills are outrageous. It never ends. And I wouldn't have it any other way.

Perhaps my friends and I are a little more fanatical about fishing than some people, but there are just as many folks who are even more fanatical than us. That's why I say the true joy in fishing is that you can dive in with both feet or take it easy and relax, and either way you have just as much fun.

Even if you take the relaxing route and fish to enjoy some moments of tranquility, you will still benefit from learning a little about the fish and their environments. Just being in the places where fish are found can't help but stir that inner naturalist in us. You see birds, hear frogs, smell fragrant cedars; freed from the sterility of the urban wasteland, your senses come alive on the water. The stimulation awakens your brain, and you become curious about the wondrous things that might be happening below the water's surface. And it seldom takes long before you begin to ask yourself when you're going to get a bite. The point of going fishing is, after all, to catch fish. So how do we do that?

Many people associate fishing success with luck. True, there is an element of luck in fishing. We've all heard stories of some kid on a dock catching a whopper while the seasoned pro goes home empty-handed. But luck is a one-shot affair—let's see the kid on the dock beat the pro three days out of five. It won't happen. Consistent results come only as a result of learning a thing or two about the fish you want to catch. If you do the right things in the right places at the right times, more often than not you'll catch fish. And by the law of averages you'll get your share of big ones, too.

The aim of this book is to help you stack the odds in your favor by exploring these wonderful creatures we call fish. We'll look at the places fish call home, as well as the bait and tackle we use to catch them. We'll discuss fishing spots and fishing techniques, and at the risk of being just a touch overconfident, we'll even look at how to fillet your catch. By the time you reach the back cover, you'll be able to venture onto any body of water and, within a reasonable length of time, catch some very nice fish.

You'll also find that the basics of fishing are transferable from one type of fish to another. An angler who travels around North America often finds that the skills used to catch fish at home can prove equally valuable on the opposite side of the continent. A southern U.S. largemouth-bass angler will find Ontario smallmouth aren't too much different, just as an east coast brook-trout angler will feel right at home on a Vancouver Island steelhead stream. Perhaps that's part of the reason fishing seems to have such widespread appeal.

I believe the celebrated novelist Robert Traver put it best: "It isn't that fishing is so terribly important," he wrote. "But so many other things in life are equally unimportant, and not nearly so much fun." Amen.

CHAPTER 1

About Fish

The average human being has a brain that's a little bigger than a good-sized grapefruit. The average freshwater fish, on the other hand, has a brain about the size of a pea. So why is it that fish so often elude capture?

Let's face it—we're talking about a creature that's so far down the evolutionary totem pole, it hasn't even crawled up onto land yet. It shouldn't be that hard to outsmart it. And yet, all too often, people go fishing and come home empty-handed. Why?

The majority of car accidents result from what the insurance companies like to call "operator error," and that term aptly describes the reasons

Sometimes referred to as the water wolf, the northern pike is the top predator throughout its range.

people don't catch more fish: we screw up. Any predator worth its salt knows a thing or two about the prey it tries to capture. Yet we often head off on a fishing expedition with no real knowledge about the fish we want to catch. We pick a spot at random, chuck out a bait, and wait for something to happen. And as we often find out, relying on luck sure doesn't put many fish on our stringer.

True, there is great pleasure in the simple act of fishing. It's great to be outside in beautiful surroundings, hearing the happy songs of birds, or the haunting cry of a loon, absorbing the soothing tranquility of calm water. But the point of fishing is, after all, to catch fish. And to do that with any degree of consistency, we really do need to take a good hard look at these creatures we call fish.

Fish aren't intelligent, but they are predictable creatures of habit, with basic needs. Once you understand what these needs are, you can accurately and consistently predict not only where fish can be found but also how they will respond to lures and baits on any given day, regardless of the weather. With that knowledge, you can arrange to be on the water when the conditions are best and make the most of the time available to you.

Fish are truly remarkable animals in that their basic design hasn't changed much in hundreds of thousands of years. Yet fish come in an incredibly diverse range of shapes, colors, and sizes. Trying to define just what constitutes a fish is a difficult exercise, because no matter how basic the criteria you try to work with, there seems to be at least one exception to every rule.

We could say that all fish breathe with gills. But the African lungfish can gulp air and "breathe" with its air bladder, which functions like a primitive lung. It is this ability that allows the lungfish to survive extended droughts. They burrow deep in the mud and gulp air, surviving weeks or even months till the rains come and re-flood their dried-up pond or stream.

We could say that all fish swim in water. But the walking catfish, a unique species found in Florida, can walk over dry land on its stiff pectoral fins. They're sometimes seen crossing roads as they wander from one pond to the next. You wouldn't think of fish as possible roadkill, but in Florida's Everglades country drivers do occasionally collide with a walking catfish.

We could say that fish are covered with scales—but that's really not true either. Carp have big coarse scales the size of golf balls, while brook trout are covered in ultra-fine scales more like the heads of pins. And catfish have no scales at all.

Fish range in size from tiny minnows an inch long to the giant whale shark, which reaches sixty feet (18 m) in length. Some, like the salmon, swim quickly, turn on a dime, and leap clear of the water, while others, like the giant ocean sunfish, can barely manage forward motion at all. So, from an angler's perspective, what can we say about fish that will facilitate our task of understanding them?

Scientists tell us that regardless of the species, all fish respond to four basic things: comfort, food, reproduction, and predation. I can assure you that one of those four elements plays a hand in the location of every fish you will ever catch, anywhere in the world.

Comfort, to a fish, means water that is within a certain temperature range. Fish are cold-blooded animals, and every fish has a range of water temperature within which its body systems function most efficiently. Comfort also involves things like light intensity. Fish don't have eyelids, so they can't blink. I've never seen one wearing Ray-Bans either, so if the sun grows too strong, they duck under some shade or go deeper, to a point where the water filters light to a more tolerable level. If things grow too noisy with passing boats and water skiers, fish don't throw on a classical CD and listen to it through headphones. Again, they move to a new location where there's less racket.

Food is straightforward. Fish need to eat to survive, so they'll never be far from some source of nourishment. Their needs associated with *reproduction* are equally simple to understand. At least once each year, that basic need to do the hokeypokey with others of their kind will concentrate fish into predictable locations in a lake or river.

Smallmouth bass have small mouths only in comparison to a largemouth. Greenish-brown in coloration and covered with numerous thin vertical bars, they're fierce predators that can thrive in both lakes and rivers.

Finally, *predation* also affects fish location. With the exception of the very largest pike, muskie, lake trout, and salmon, freshwater fish face a variety of predators, and so will hang out in places that afford some degree of protection from becoming someone else's next lunch. To a fish, nothing ruins a day like crossing paths with an otter.

So, one truth that applies to *all* fish is that they tend to do things for specific reasons. Fish exist on the level of basic common sense. One of the hardest jobs for a budding angler is to cultivate that common-sense thinking.

North American anglers are truly blessed with a wide variety of so-called game species to fish for, including several types of trout, six species of salmon, three members each of the pike and perch families, freshwater bass and other members of the sunfish family, as well as a variety of so-called non-sporting fish such as carp, catfish, and freshwater drum. The term "game fish" goes back to at least the seventeenth century, when some enterprising angler with too much time on his hands decided that since people seemed to fit neatly into different social classes, fish should too. Game fish, then, would include the "desirable" species—the ones the rich preferred to catch—while the less desirable species, dubbed coarse fish, were left for the common folk. This silly concept is outdated and, quite frankly, utter nonsense. I quite like catching several coarse or non-game species such as carp and freshwater drum, while an entire industry has grown around catfishing, including fancy catfish rods, catfish baits, catfish hooks, tournaments, magazines—the works. So much for not being worthy of a true angler's time.

Angler preference for particular species is very much linked to geography, reflecting the natural distribution of different fish species across the continent. In eastern Canada and the northeastern United States, trout, salmon, smallmouth bass, and chain pickerel are the fish most often pursued, while in the southern states it's catfish and largemouth bass. Through the Prairies, walleye and pike command the angler's attention, while the mountains and Pacific coast are trout and salmon territory. To the far north, lake trout and Arctic char reign supreme.

Perhaps the luckiest anglers in all of North America are those who live in the Midwest/Great Lakes region, where all of these geographic ranges overlap to some degree. Anglers here may not have the very best fishing for any one species, but they enjoy pretty darned good fishing for just about everything.

Of course, humankind's intervention has changed things considerably, and thanks to hatchery stocking programs it is now possible to catch a variety of fish species thousands of miles beyond their natural home range, including Atlantic salmon on the Pacific coast, Florida-strain largemouth bass in California lakes, even saltwater striped bass in fresh-water impoundments. An Oregon angler fishing the Columbia River is as likely to catch walleye as salmon, and muskie are showing up in places they've never been seen before.

This artificial introduction of fish into new waters has had mixed results. In some cases, such as the stocking of Pacific salmon in the Great Lakes or the release of Atlantic striped bass into San Francisco Bay, these introductions have led to the development of exciting new fisheries where none existed before. But in other cases, as in the accidental introduction of grass carp to North America or the arrival of round gobies and river ruffe in the Great Lakes through the discharge of ballast water by foreign ships, the introductions have proven disastrous as the exotic invaders displaced native species.

All fish species have the same basic senses of smell, vision, sensitivity to vibration, and sensitivity to temperature. Some types of fish have more evolved senses than others, which affects where we will find them and how we might go about catching them. Pike and muskie, for example, have a highly developed sense of sight. Accordingly, they're almost always found in clear water, hunting prey visually. Fish for them in a murky lake and you'll probably come home empty-handed. Given the way they've evolved, fishing highly visible lures in clear lakes and rivers is the best way to catch them.

The mighty sturgeon represents the opposite end of the scale. These prehistoric-looking fish have a superb sense of smell and touch, and normally forage along the bottom, finding food (including dead stuff) by scent using highly sensitive barbels that hang around the perimeter of the mouth. Their highly developed senses of smell and touch allow sturgeon to thrive in waters murkier than a pike could ever survive in. Although sturgeon have reasonable vision, they certainly don't need it to feed and flourish.

There are times when fish will take advantage of abrupt changes in water clarity in order to feed. One of the best examples can be found on any lake in the summer when you have a strong onshore wind blowing on a sandy shoreline. The waves dislodge sediment, mudding the water along the shoreline. They also unearth a variety of small bottom organisms like crayfish, creating a unique feeding opportunity for fish of all sizes. Really big fish will hide in the cloudy water, just waiting for a smaller fish to appear in the murk. Or they may sit out in the clear water, waiting for a smaller fish to pop out into the open. In this situation the fish use cloudy water as cover; they're still sight-feeding, but in cloudy water. It's rather weird, but very common.

All fish have a highly developed sensitivity to vibration, which takes the place of human hearing. Although fish certainly can hear and do have ears, they depend far more on their vibrational sense to warn them of approaching predators or to betray the presence of prey. Fish sense vibration with their lateral line—a continuous line of nerve endings found along each side of the fish, from the gill cover to the base of the tail. Some types of fishing lures appeal to this sense by generating enticing thumping vibrations that arouse curiosity or duplicate patterns made by prey species. Because water is so much better a conductor of vibration than air, this sense is highly developed in most fish species. It's also the reason that quiet, stealthy anglers catch far more fish.

Several years ago I was sitting on the bank of southern Ontario's Ganaraska River with a good friend, Greg Elaschuk, stuffing down a sandwich and drinking a pop, enjoying the warm sunshine of an early May morning. The Ganaraska is a very popular trout river about an hour or so from Toronto, so we weren't particularly surprised to see two other anglers walking up the path that followed the stream bank. They were clearly headed for the deep, slow pool where we had been fishing most of the morning.

The two anglers splashed across the river so they could approach from the opposite side. This route took them through a rather large patch of soft mud where, to our amusement, they both sank up to their knees and had quite a tough time getting through. On emerging from the tar pit, they proceeded to kick a convenient log to get the mud off their waders, dump a bag of gear they had been carrying on the ground, then stomp their way to the edge of the river, where they stood in clear view of the fish. Although the river is only about fifty feet (15 m) wide at this point, they were wearing chest-high waders, so they must have felt they just had to wade in, kicking up rocks and leaving great clouds of sediment behind them. One of the two saw us perched on the opposite bank, waved, and asked how the fishing was. That's when his partner shushed him harshly and reminded him they had to be quiet to avoid frightening the fish. It was hard to keep from laughing out loud, as virtually every fish for a hundred miles must have heard them coming.

There's no question fish can hear airborne sounds. Go for a swim and have someone talk while your head's underwater—you can hear every word. If you have a boat with a radio or a CD player in it, turn it on and go for a swim. Underwater the sound gets a little bit distorted, but you can hear it from a surprising distance.

Whether or not airborne sounds arouse a fish's sense of alarm is another matter. One of my fishing buddies is a real loudmouth, yet for all his bellowing he catches a lot of fish, so it doesn't appear to bother them. But noise associated with vibration will definitely send every fish around into hiding, and pronto. Drop a pair of pliers on the bottom of an aluminum boat and you may as well set off depth charges; the effect will be the same. Fish are especially sensitive to vibrations in very shallow water or over a rocky bottom. Whereas a soft bottom or abundant weed growth can cushion sound, a hard bottom will amplify it.

Another characteristic common to all fish is that they show a clear preference for water in a given temperature range. Being cold-blooded, a fish's metabolism is controlled by the temperature of the water around it. A fish in cold water will tend to be less active than the same fish in warmer water. But each species has a temperature range within which its systems function most effectively. Trout and salmon, for instance, are most comfortable in cold water, generally somewhere from 48 to 60°F (9–16°C). Largemouth bass, on the other hand, are happiest in much warmer water; 75 to 80°F (24–27°C) is a perfect temperature for them. Smallmouth bass, walleye, perch, and pike prefer temperatures that are somewhere in between. The point, of course, is that you won't find many fish in water that's well outside their preferred temperature range. Although they can certainly survive in hotter or colder conditions, fish will move to find water that is more comfortable. This is an important consideration for an angler and is one reason that you'll find most fishing stores selling pocket thermometers and electronic temperature gauges.

In short, all fish respond in some way to certain basic sensations. Now, let's take a much more in-depth look at the more popular freshwater fish in North America and see how they differ from one another.

Trout

Anglers have pursued trout since humans lived in caves. Although the use of clubs and spears is now considered somewhat unsporting, we still pursue trout with intense passion. And happily for us, North America offers some of the very best trout fishing in the world.

There are in fact two different groups of fish that are lumped together in the trout family, namely, true trout and char. True trout, including the rainbow trout, brown trout, and cutthroat trout, have long cylindrical bodies with one soft-rayed fin on the back, a terminal mouth with well-developed, conical teeth, five soft-rayed belly fins, and a powerful tail. On the back, between the tail and the dorsal fin, is a small, fleshy appendage called an adipose fin.

Regardless of species, all true trout feature dark-colored spots against a lighter-colored body. This separates them from the char, including the lake trout, brook trout, bull trout, Arctic char, and Dolly Varden, which have a similarly shaped body but sport light-colored spots against a darker background. There are other taxonomic differences, but unless you're really into biology it doesn't matter. Both trout and char are fun to catch and superb on a dinner plate.

Rainbow trout are undoubtedly the most widely distributed species, thanks in no small part to hatchery stocking programs. Rainbows are among the most adaptable fish in the world, and this is often reflected in their appearance. They seem to come in every possible color and shape, which leads to tremendous confusion among anglers and, sometimes, biologists. However, regardless of external color, all rainbows can be identified by backs and tails covered with small black dots, which on the tail radiate outwards in neat, even rows, and mouths that are completely white inside.

Cutthroat trout, which get their name from the brilliant red slash mark found beneath their jaws, exhibit almost as wide a range of appearance as rainbows. A fish of the Rocky Mountains and Pacific coast, cutts have not been introduced widely outside their native range, at least not to anywhere near the same degree as rainbows.

Cutts are bright, lively, beautiful fish that are always a delight to catch. Although they've been known to reach forty pounds (18 kg), most weigh two pounds (0.9 kg) or less, with the biggest always coming from remote alpine lakes. The key to identifying them is the

Guide Victor Gagnon (left) helps angler Siegfried Gagnon come to grips with a magnificent, four-pound (1.8-kg) Quebec brook trout.

Dan Ralph is all smiles over his trophy brown trout.

Rainbow trout from small streams and lakes are typically dark above, with silver sides peppered with small black dots, and a pink blush extending along the flanks and gill covers.

Lake trout are typically gray to black all over, and peppered with small, white spots. No other member of the trout and salmon family has such a deeply forked tail.

Rainbow Trout

red slash under the jaw. Sea-run cutthroats are relatively abundant along the Pacific coast, reaching up to four pounds (1.8 kg) in size. They're one of the most beautiful fish in the sea, with silvery yellow flanks covered all over with pronounced black spots.

There is far less variability in the appearance of brown trout. Native to the United Kingdom and Europe, browns were introduced to North America in the late 1800s. Shy and elusive, a big brown trout is considered quite a catch, particularly when taken from a small stream.

Brown trout in rivers are butter yellow to a cream color along the sides, with prominent black spots along the back and flanks. Some fish also show pronounced red spots along the sides. There are few if any spots on the tail. Stream fish typically weigh from one to two pounds (0.5–1 kg), but they can reach astonishing weights even in tiny creeks. I know of one fish weighing in excess of eleven pounds (5 kg), which came from a creek so narrow that most adults could straddle it.

24

Brown trout in lakes are often huge, particularly in the case of big waters like the Great Lakes or some of the big reservoirs in the southwestern United States, like the legendary Flaming Gorge system on the Utah–Wyoming border. There, browns often grow so fat that anglers call them footballs, and they can weigh more than thirty pounds (14 kg). The present angling record is just shy of forty-five pounds (20 kg). Lake-resident brown trout tend to be paler, silvery along the sides, with large, round, dark spots on the gill cover and occasionally dark x-shaped marks along the flanks.

Lake trout, actually a type of char, are the largest members of the trout/char family. The biggest recorded to date was a massive 102-pound (46 kg) monster caught by a commercial fisherman in northern Saskatchewan's Lake Athabasca in the 1960s. Slow-growing and long-lived, lake trout in remote northern lakes frequently top twenty pounds (9 kg); in the best waters, fifty-pounders (23 kg) are caught every year. They seldom reach such sizes in more southerly lakes, though they still average a respectable five pounds (2.3 kg) or so.

Lake trout are fish of deep, cold lakes. Extremely intolerant of warm water, they spend their summers in depths of a hundred feet (30 m) or more, where their pewter gray to black bodies, peppered with white spots, virtually disappear in the shadows. No other trout or salmon has a tail as deeply forked as a laker, and this fork is often the first thing an angler sees while battling the fish to the surface. Like all trout and char, lake trout have exceptional vision and a finely developed lateral line.

Brook trout are found in streams, big rivers, and lakes, with the larger fish normally coming from lakes and very big rivers. Brook trout demand cold, clean water and do poorly in anything less than a pristine habitat. They do occasionally run down to the sea, where they take on a silvery appearance. Most brookies found in streams weigh less than a pound (0.5 kg), while lake fish may reach four or five pounds (1.8–2.3 kg). The biggest to date was a fourteen-pound (6.4 kg) giant caught in Ontario's Nipigon River.

Bull trout and Dolly Varden were once considered to be the same species. Biologists have now determined that populations of this fish found along the Pacific coast are classified as Dolly Varden char (named for a character in a Charles Dickens novel), while those found along the eastern slope of the Rockies are to be called bull trout. Both bull trout and Dolly Varden appear dull gray in color, with the typical char-type white spots peppering the sides. A century ago they were subject to bounties in many areas; now they're the focus of species recovery projects. Although relatively easy to catch, these fish do not enjoy the same popularity as rainbow and cutthroat trout. They're not as pretty, they don't jump when hooked, and they are still hated in many areas for their habit of gorging upon newly hatched salmon fry.

Arctic char are considered to be among the most beautiful fish in fresh water, as evidenced by this large male from the Tree River in Canada's Northwest Territories.

Arctic char are widely distributed across a big chunk of northern Canada, but they are found in such remote places that they're of limited interest to anglers. Brilliant silver with white spots along the sides, they turn blood-red at spawning time, their bodies covered with white spots, making them among the most striking of all freshwater fish. Landlocked populations are found in some lakes in eastern Quebec, where they're sometimes referred to as Quebec red trout. Where ocean-going fish may reach thirty pounds (14 kg) or more, landlocked Arctic char seldom top five pounds (2.3 kg).

Salmon

The fish of kings, salmon are native to the east and west coasts of North America. Atlantic salmon typically range from four to forty pounds (1.8–18 kg). Fresh from the sea, they're brilliant silver with large dark spots along the back, gill covers, and upper part of the flanks. As they approach spawning time, the fish take on a duller brown hue, with the lower jaw of the males often developing a pronounced upward hook called a kype. They're known for their incredible strength, including their propensity to jump. In fact, their scientific name, *Salmo salar*, means just that—the leaper.

Atlantic Salmon

Landlocked populations of Atlantic salmon, called ouananiche in eastern Canada, are found in clear lakes from New Hampshire to Labrador and northern Quebec. These landlocked fish never reach the size of their sea-run kin but are every bit as respected as sport fish. Very much a fish of pristine, clean environments, they're exceptionally beautiful and tremendously strong. Most weigh from three to six pounds (1.4–2.7 kg), but they can reach twenty pounds (9 kg) or more.

Whether landlocked or sea-run, Atlantic salmon have stiff tails that will not compress under pressure, allowing them to be easily carried by gripping your hand around the base of the tail. This has become the preferred way to land hooked salmon as it minimizes handling. You can even buy commercially made tailers, which look somewhat like a cross between a noose and a buggy whip.

Along the Pacific coast we have five species of salmon to contend with; of these, two are of prime interest to anglers. The biggest—the chinook, also known as the spring or king salmon—can top ninety-five pounds (43 kg) and destroy all but the strongest tackle. Adult chinook average twenty to thirty pounds (9–14 kg), and have been introduced around the globe. Today they're abundant throughout the Great Lakes and have been introduced to several large prairie reservoirs in the United States. They're also now found in the coastal rivers of Chile and New Zealand.

Chinook Salmon

Though smaller in size, coho salmon—which still average a healthy ten to twelve pounds (4.5–5.5 kg) and often top twenty (9 kg)—are one of the most popular fish in the Pacific. They jump wildly when hooked, often leaping out of the water repeatedly in crazed, head-over-tail frenzies. Pound for pound, few fish can match a coho for sheer brute strength. Coho are the fish responsible for the rebirth of the Great Lakes as a sport fishing paradise, and they remain an angler's favorite there today.

Also found along the Pacific coast are sockeye, chum, and pink salmon. These shrimp and plankton eaters, mainly left to the commercial fleet, have only recently been discovered by anglers. But as anglers develop techniques to catch them, entire new frontiers are opening up. Fly fishing for these exciting fish is a growing sport, particularly in brackish water at river mouths.

Kokanee, which are a landlocked sockeye salmon, are quite abundant and extremely popular in big deep lakes along the Pacific slope of the Rocky Mountains. Though they generally weigh only from one to two pounds (0.5–1 kg), kokanee are a superb sport fish, offering a wild fight that's way out of proportion to their size. Most are caught by trolling slowly with small spoons.

Pike

Three members of this exciting fish family are of interest to anglers: the northern pike, the chain pickerel, and the muskellunge. With long thin bodies, duck-like mouths studded with razor-sharp teeth, and fins set well to the rear, these are superbly adapted ambush predators and among the most exciting fish in fresh water.

Northern pike are one of the most widely distributed fish in the world, found throughout the northern hemisphere. Pike thrive equally well in lakes and rivers, where they eat just about anything they can catch. Most pike caught by anglers weigh from two to six pounds (1–2.7 kg), but much

Pike

larger fish are taken regularly. A good pike will measure three feet (1 m) in length and weigh from ten to twelve pounds (4.5–5.5 kg), while fish of forty inches (100 cm) in length and weighing in excess of sixteen pounds (7 kg) are considered trophies. Huge pike may top forty pounds (18 kg). Today the largest North American pike consistently come from remote lakes in northern Canada, where they face limited fishing pressure.

An intriguing characteristic of pike is that their preferred habitat changes profoundly with the onset of sexual maturity. Juvenile pike favor shallow weedbeds, where they eagerly attack just about anything that moves, including each other. But as the fish reach adulthood and attain weights of seven to eight pounds (3.2–3.6 kg), they become denizens of cold, deep water. Big pike won't hesitate to move as deep as seventy to ninety feet (21–27 m) in summer, where they feed on large prey like whitefish and small lake trout.

Chain pickerel are far smaller than pike, averaging two to four pounds (0.9–1.8 kg) and occasionally reaching six to seven pounds (2.7–3.2 kg). Common throughout eastern Canada and the northeastern United States, they're often mistaken for immature pike.

The pike's bigger cousin, the muskellunge, is another kettle of fish altogether. Capable of reaching weights in excess of sixty pounds (27 kg) and averaging fifteen to twenty pounds (6.8–9 kg), muskie are among the most feared predators in fresh water.

Tiger muskie, a sterile hybrid created by crossing a muskellunge and a northern pike, occur occasionally in nature and have been widely introduced in put-and-take fisheries through hatchery production. These striking fish are rather light colored with small, extremely pronounced vertical bars all along the body. The epithet "tiger" is quite fitting.

Perch

The perch family contains three members that are of interest to anglers: the yellow perch, the sauger, and the walleye.

Yellow perch are unmistakable, with their brilliant yellow bodies covered with dark vertical bars. Averaging about six inches (15 cm) in length but reaching thirteen inches (33 cm) or more, perch roam lakes and rivers in huge schools. Almost everything in the water eats perch, so apart from being of direct interest to anglers as a game species, they're also important as a source of forage for other fish. Sauger look like skinny perch in shape, averaging twelve to sixteen inches (30–40 cm) in length and about a pound (half a kilogram) or so in weight.

Besides being the largest member of the perch clan, walleye are among the most popular game fish in North America. A highly adaptable fish, walleye do well in both rivers and lakes. They thrive in still waters or in fast currents, occupy areas from the extreme shallows to the depths, and may either hang tight to cover such as weeds or suspend in open water.

With their brilliant yellow coloration and numerous green bars, it's tough to mistake a yellow perch for any other species of freshwater fish.

No wonder they're so popular—there's always another new way to catch them.

That walleye are one of the most popular table fish in the world doesn't hurt either. They're the subject of an intense commercial fishery, with fresh walleye fillets fetching premium prices at fish markets here and abroad. Their flaky white meat can be prepared in a variety of ways, all of them thoroughly delicious.

Walleye are typically dark green to black on the back, with golden yellow sides, a white belly, and no spots or bars on the body. The tail is normally tipped in white at the bottom, and this is often the first thing an angler sees in the water when fighting a walleye. They have large, pronounced canine teeth, giving the fish a vampire-like appearance. Though pointy, the teeth are conical in profile and seldom cut fishing line.

The oddly named walleye has a unique silvery-colored membrane within its eye, called the *tapetum lucidum*. This membrane gives the walleye extraordinary vision in conditions of low light, making it an efficient predator at dawn, at dusk, and through the night. Clear water and brilliant sunshine often means slow fishing for walleye, as the fish bury themselves under rocks and weeds to escape the bright sun. But as soon as that light goes down—watch out.

The white spot on the bottom of a walleye's tail is often the first thing an angler sees in the water while reeling in the fish. Joe Cutajar caught this one on a jig.

29

Largemouth Bass

Bass

The fish we call bass in North America are in fact the largest members of the sunfish family. The biggest is the largemouth bass, probably the most important sporting species in North America. Entire industries exist around bass fishing: bass tournaments, bass rods and reels, bass lures, even bass boats. Think they must be fun to catch?

Largemouth bass are aptly named, for their huge mouth is so big that they're often referred to as bucketmouths, or buckets for short. Very much a fish of cover, there's no such thing as water that's too shallow or too weedy for largemouth. Some of the best bass come from weeds so thick that a person might be tempted to step out of the boat and go for a stroll.

Largemouth are fish of warm, shallow water, and for this reason they tend to do better in the southern United States than in Canada. The current world-record largemouth bass is a 22 lb., 4 oz. (10.1 kg) fish caught in Georgia in 1932. It has been said that the next world-record fish could be worth millions of dollars to the angler who catches it, paid primarily by tackle companies looking for endorsement deals. The biggest bass these days come from California, where an angler named Bob Crupi has almost broken the record on two separate occasions, boating enormous largemouth of twenty-two pounds even (10 kg) and twenty-one pounds even (9.5 kg) respectively. Needless to say, all eyes are on Mr. Crupi these days, with some people believing it is only a matter of time till he catches the next world record. Some Las Vegas casinos are reportedly offering good odds on it happening within the next five years.

Most definitely a fish of the weeds, largemouth bass are typically a dull green color, with a broad, dark stripe running the length of the fish along each flank.

Next in popularity is the smallmouth bass, which is a somewhat misleading name, for its gaping jaws are small only in comparison with those of a largemouth. They're still more than capable of eating huge meals. Smallmouth are more of a northern fish than the largemouth, and are particularly fond of clear, cool rivers and lakes. Where largemouth are very much fish of weeds, smallmouth tend to prefer more open, rocky environments. However, they're almost as adaptable as largemouth and will use whatever cover is available, including weeds if that's where the food is. Smallmouth eat virtually anything they can catch, including smaller fish, frogs, crayfish, invertebrates, leeches, and even terrestrial creatures such as mice or snakes that happen to wind up in the water. They frequently take food from the surface, to the delight of anglers everywhere.

Smallmouth often school and can become competitive when feeding. Indeed, it's not unusual to hook a good smallmouth only to find a half-dozen others of the same size following it up to the boat, hoping to steal a piece of the lure it just ate. This aggressive nature, combined with its brute strength and tendency to jump repeatedly when hooked, has led thousands of anglers to agree that the smallmouth is pound-for-pound the gamest fish that swims. They won't get any argument from me.

Spotted bass, also known as Kentucky bass, are found throughout the east-central United States. Superficially, they resemble largemouth, but they live more like smallmouth, preferring more open cover and water. Spots often travel in schools and can be fun to catch once you find them. Although they don't reach the same size as largemouth and are not as aggressive as smallies, spots have their own special charm.

Channel catfish are abundant in rivers and lakes across much of North America.

Most smaller members of the sunfish family also wind up on a hook at some point, with the bluegill and pumpkinseed sunfish, the rock bass, the black crappie, and the larger white crappie among the most frequently targeted species. Both black and white crappie are especially popular in the south, but anglers target them wherever they're found. Big ones, approaching the size and shape of a dinner plate, are often referred to as "slabs." Though these smaller fish don't fight very hard, they're great fun to catch and, despite what their name may suggest, are possibly the tastiest fish in fresh water.

Catfish

Immensely popular throughout eastern North America, the catfish family includes several important game fish. Probably the most important species is the channel catfish, which thrives in both rivers and lakes, and has a real love affair with strong currents. Indeed, the fast water at the base of waterfalls and hydroelectric dams is an ideal place to fish for channel cats, followed by log-strewn rivers where one might expect to find trout.

Channel cats average from two to eight pounds (0.9–3.6 kg) but can reach astonishing weights in waters with favorable habitat. The present all-tackle world record is listed as a fifty-eight-pound (26 kg) behemoth caught in South Carolina's Santee–Cooper Reservoir in 1964. Channel cats are a delicious table fish, so much so that they're the focus of an intense catfish farming industry. Their flaky flesh lends itself to being served in a number of ways; blackened catfish is considered a Cajun delicacy.

Channel Catfish

In the southern United States the blue cat and flathead cat provide big-game thrills for freshwater anglers. These powerful fish can reach weights in excess of 100 pounds (45 kg) and may average twice the weight of channel cats. Both are voracious predators and first-class sport, even on heavy tackle.

Bullhead represent the opposite end of the catfish spectrum, averaging a pound (0.5 kg) or less apiece and rarely topping four pounds (1.8 kg). Most abundant is the brown bullhead, a small, sluggish inhabitant of shallow, weedy water. Towards the south the black bullhead and yellow bull-head are also abundant. Bullheads swarm into shallow water to spawn each spring, and in some places anglers descend on marshes by night to harvest these fish by the pailful. Though they may look rather homely, bullheads are superb table fish.

Carp

It amazes me how a fish that is widely revered as a magnificent game species in one country can be contemptuously dismissed as a garbage fish in another. Yet that is precisely the case with carp. Perhaps the number one sport fish in the U.K. and Europe, they've traditionally been considered little more than swimming fertilizer in North America. Happily, that attitude is slowly changing.

It's tough to argue against carp. They reach enormous sizes—they often average a healthy ten to fifteen pounds (4.5–6.8 kg) and frequently top thirty (13.6 kg)—fight like demons, and seem to thrive in urban waterways that won't support many other kinds of fish, creating big-game fishing opportunities quite close to home for millions of city-dwelling anglers. The largest members of the minnow family and a close relative of the common goldfish, carp have been known to surpass eighty pounds (36 kg). In Germany people give them as Christmas presents.

Carp can be found throughout eastern North America. They thrive equally in lakes, big rivers, and ponds, feeding on a variety of matter while foraging along the bottom in shallow water. They have superbly developed senses of smell and taste, so most carp angling involves still fishing with organic baits of some sort. Most carp angling takes place in the early summer, when the fish concentrate in shallow marshy areas to spawn.

Freshwater Drum

Sometimes called sheepshead, freshwater drum are a member of the croaker family, which includes a large number of popular saltwater game fish. Freshwater drum are omnivores that gobble up a variety of prey, including insects, invertebrates, crayfish, smaller fish, and sometimes vegetation. They often hit lures intended for other species and put up a grand fight when hooked. Landing a big one, especially on light tackle, is no easy feat. Most weigh from four to eight pounds (1.8–3.6 kg), but much larger specimens are caught from time to time. The present world record is listed as an enormous fifty-four pound (24 kg) fish, caught in 1972 from a lake in Tennessee.

A fish of big waters, freshwater drum thrive in large rivers and lakes. They are surprisingly tolerant of turbidity but prefer clear environments. Drum are also remarkably tolerant of man and often thrive in urban water bodies. For city-based anglers willing to look for them, they can provide great fishing very close to home.

CHAPTER 2

Picking a Fishing Spot

The first time you stand on the end of a dock, fishing rod in hand, staring out at a wide-open lake, you can't help but wonder—where the heck do you start?

One of the realities of fishing is that you can have a $60,000 boat, a $1,000 rod and reel, a $40 custom-made lure, the best technique in the world—and none of it matters if you're in the wrong place. Unlike the fish in your aquarium at home, fish in a lake or river do not distribute themselves evenly throughout the water. They tend to concentrate in specific locations at specific times, as they address their basic needs of food, comfort, protection, and reproduction. There's an old saying that 90 percent of the fish sit in 10 percent of the water, and that's very close to the truth. Learn to identify that magical 10 percent and you will catch a lot of fish.

Beaver lodges can be extremely productive providing they sit adjacent to deep water. Sunken branches provide wonderful spots for big fish to ambush prey.

So just what constitutes a good fishing spot? The answer to that question depends largely on what kind of fish you're trying to catch. A spot that's ideal for lake trout might be completely wrong for largemouth bass. But happily, there are some generalities that always seem to apply, whether you're fishing in a lake, river, or reservoir.

Going back to those basic needs that all fish share, food is the single greatest factor affecting their location. Wild creatures like fish will never be located far from their next meal. Find the greatest concentration of prey items and you will find the predatory fish. In one sense you're not so much looking to find spots that will appeal to the fish you're trying to catch as trying to find spots that will be home to their natural prey.

Shorelines

In lakes, reservoirs, and large rivers the most fertile waters are the shallows. These areas, which biologists refer to as the littoral zone, burst with life: plants, insects, crustaceans, amphibians, small fish, and big fish too. If we think of a lake as a fish's house, the shallows are the kitchen.

Many types of fish will feed in, or adjacent to, shallow water. Shallow is a relative term, of course, and water clarity plays a role in determining just what constitutes shallow water. For an angler's purposes the shallows are anywhere you can see bottom—normally somewhere between one and ten feet (30 cm and 3 m).

The most obvious areas of shallow water on any lake are the shorelines. Apart from offering shallow, fertile water, shorelines represent a physical barrier to the fish. Occasionally, fish will even make use of the shoreline to corner prey. Smallmouth bass, and to a lesser degree walleye, are notorious for herding fish, tadpoles, and other unfortunate creatures up against lake shorelines, particularly in clear Canadian Shield lakes, which tend to be relatively infertile.

The most spectacular example of this that I've ever witnessed occurred on Lac Beauchêne in western Quebec. I was fishing with Bob Izumi, host of television's *Real Fishing Show*, and his guest, Jack Lynn Heritage, the marketing person for Pradco, the company that manufactures Rebel, Heddon, Cordell, Bomber, and numerous other popular brands of fishing lures. Lac Beauchêne is a large, deep lake separated into two equal-sized parts by shallow S-shaped narrows. It was in these narrows that we witnessed an incredible smallmouth bass feeding frenzy. The still water surface came alive as literally dozens of smallmouth erupted at once, chasing baitfish and turning an area perhaps the size of a house into a cauldron of boils and splashes. In Lac Beauchêne's clear water we could clearly see the smallmouth darting at minnows just beneath the surface. These intense attacks, which we witnessed at least two dozen times over a two-hour period, lasted upwards of two or three minutes apiece.

What made it even more spectacular was the fact that eight or nine common mergansers began joining in the fray. Every time the bass herded the hapless baitfish to the surface, the mergansers would immediately dive right into the middle of the roiling water, taking advantage of the opportunity to get in on the action. The baitfish were beat—mergansers attacking them from above, smallmouth bass from below. I'd never seen anything remotely like it and doubt I ever will again.

Another time, while fishing for early spring pike on northern Saskatchewan's Wapata Lake, I saw a similar occurrence. We were fishing in a shallow, weedy bay, shaped like a big cone, which terminated in a marshy creek only inches deep. I was having a ball catching pike on almost every cast, yet the sight of huge wakes slicing across the mouth of the creek eventually got to me, and I just had to go see what was going on. To my amazement, at least two dozen enormous northerns—some of them approaching four feet (1.2 m) in length—had herded a school of minnows into the very shallow water at the creek mouth. Every time one of the minnows tried to break for deeper water, one of the pike would shoot up into the shallows and nail it. The water was so shallow that the pike frequently sliced the surface with their dorsal fins, just like sharks. It was an amazing sight, and I remember feeling very happy I was not a minnow.

So, fish do use shorelines as barriers in hunting prey. While it is, admittedly, unusual to see groups of fish corralling prey as those pike and smallmouth did, no doubt individual fish use shorelines to run down their dinner.

Shorelines are also places where fish can find other potential meals, including insects, caterpillars, frogs, snakes, and anything else that happens to tumble into the water. In some situations fish become quite focused on feeding upon terrestrial creatures that tumble into the water by accident. This is precisely why smallmouth bass love to hide in the nooks and crannies at the base of steep bluffs, where vertical rock walls plunge into lakes. It's also why trout patrol shorelines where vegetation hangs over the water. Every now and then, mother nature presents a banquet from above.

Even a small lake represents one heck of a lot of shoreline to fish. Top anglers narrow their search by looking for spots that offer something just a little different from everywhere else. Typically, that's some combination of structure and cover.

Structure and Cover

Structure is a term used to describe physical features on the bottom of the lake that attract fish, such as a reef, a shoal, a steep drop-off, a small island, or perhaps a long rocky point extending into the lake. *Cover*, on the other hand, is used to describe stuff found *on top of* the structure, like weeds or sunken logs. To put it in human terms, structure would be a particular room within a house and cover would be the furniture. Fish might call a

Points that extend towards the main lake basin are one of the most obvious shoreline hot spots.

given reef home, and gravitate towards a particular patch of weeds on the end of the reef, just as you or I would spend most our time in our living room and gravitate towards a particular chair.

If you think of your fishing locations in this way, it becomes very easy to quickly identify potential hot spots. You'll soon find yourself looking at shorelines and thinking, Geez, that spot has all the right things, or Wow, this area's pretty barren. Now you're doing something called *structure fishing*, and it's one of the keys to catching fish consistently.

Some of the better structural elements to look out for include points, islands, shoals, steep drop-offs, narrows, river mouths, bays, and saddles. Points provide some of the most obvious structure in many lakes. Any long finger of rock or sand extending out into the main lake basin will attract fish. As a general rule, the more significant the point, the more fish it will attract. Points seem to disorient fish as they move along a shoreline. The sudden change in direction represented by the point interrupts their path, and gives them an opportunity to ambush prey, especially if the point extends into deeper water.

The best rocky points will have stones of various sizes, as opposed to rocks of consistent mass. An ideal point might feature boulders from the size of a toaster to that of a car, while a poor point would consist of nothing more than an endless sea of baseball-sized rocks. Variety in stone size means more variety in the types of creatures the area can provide a home for.

Coves and inlets along the shoreline also attract their share of fish.

Like points, coves, bays, and inlets also seem to disorient fish that are cruising along the shore, causing them to pause while they sort things out. Shallow, weedy bays are normally great places to find cover-loving fish like largemouth bass and northern pike, while deeper bays attract structure-oriented fish like trout, smallmouth bass, walleye, and muskie. Any extra features in a given bay or inlet, such as a point or finger of weeds at the bay entrance, an abrupt depth change or some sunken trees, would be a key spot—the furniture in our living room, as it were.

Another wonderfully consistent shoreline spot on lakes is the mouth of any inflowing rivers or creeks. Inflowing rivers represent a source of nutrients and oxygen, so they attract fish. The water flowing into the lake may be of a higher or lower temperature than the lake itself, which can also serve to attract fish—especially in summer and winter, when water temperatures are extremely warm or cold. Predatory fish like pike, muskie, and lake trout will station themselves at river mouths to intercept smaller fish that use the river for spawning, such as trout, shiners, and suckers. Still other species, including walleye and smallmouth bass, will use the inflowing current itself for both spawning and feeding.

Once you've located several prospects based upon the structure they appear to have, it's time to look more closely at the spot and see what kind of cover there is; in human terms, is this apartment furnished or not? Cover, again, is the stuff found on the bottom, and includes weeds, sunken trees, and such.

Cover comes in two forms: *emergent*, meaning it sticks up above the water's surface, and *submerged*, which is entirely underwater. Emergent cover, including weeds like bulrush, water lily, and arrowhead, fallen trees, or even things like boat docks, is tops for attracting shallow-water fish like largemouth bass, sunfish, perch, and smaller northern pike. Submerged cover, including weeds like milfoil, coontail, and pondweed (which many anglers call "cabbage"), as well as sunken stumps and logs, attracts fish like walleye, smallmouth bass, big largemouth bass, crappie, pike, and muskie—fish that tend to like a little more water over their back. In either case, the best cover will be broken and open, as opposed to a continuous, never-ending field of solid vegetation. Fish don't like to exert any more effort than necessary in moving around, so open channels and pockets that facilitate navigation are always a plus.

Something to bear in mind is that some spots will be better at certain times of day. Some locations will produce the most action early and late in the day, when trees along the shoreline cast long shadows on the water and the shade encourages fish to hunt. That shade may also come from walls of high, submerged vegetation. Other spots may be better when the

Finding fish in smaller creeks is simply a matter of finding water deep enough for them to hide in. Undercut bank areas or spots where the current has eroded holes under overhanging trees can be a top spot.

sun is directly overhead, the warmth of its rays making fish come alive. Warm-water species like bass and muskie are usually at their best once the sun's rays have warmed the water. On the other hand, cool-water fish like walleye and trout tend to be most active when shade helps cool the water.

Offshore Structure

While the shallows may represent the most fertile part of any lake, not all types of fish use them. Fish are opportunistic. If there are meals to be found offshore, away from the shorelines, you can bet the farm that at least some big predatory fish will be out there making hay.

Some species of fish simply aren't structure-oriented. They may move offshore into deeper water to take advantage of feeding opportunities or to escape bright sunlight. After all, the deeper you go, the darker things get, and since fish have neither eyelids nor expensive Ray-Bans, those species that don't like bright light invariably spend the daylight hours in deeper water. Other fish may prefer the cooler temperatures found in the depths.

Fishing pressure can also move fish away from the shorelines. On lakes that receive a lot of angler attention or see a lot of boat traffic, you face a double whammy: not only do some fish leave the shorelines for quieter areas, but those that stay behind become extremely gun-shy. On heavily fished lakes these creatures see so many lures and baits, they can be almost impossible to fool. While participating in a bass tournament on northwestern Ontario's Lake of the Woods a few years ago, I watched at least four boats in succession fish the same weedy point over a period of about an hour and a half. I shudder to think of how many people must have fished that spot over the entire weekend. Think the fish there have learned a thing or two about what to avoid eating?

Not so with those less obvious fishing spots located off the shoreline. The best places to start are offshore shoals, reefs, and humps, where the bottom rises to form a submerged island of sorts. This reef may consist of various-sized boulders, sand, gravel, or bedrock. The rules of differentiating good shoreline features from poor ones also apply to offshore structures. The bigger the shoal or reef, the better. Similarly, those with rocks of various sizes beat those with more uniform bottoms. Reefs and shoals with cover on them, such as clumps of submerged weeds or emergent vegetation like bulrush, are always better bets than those with clean bottoms.

My favorite type of shoal is called a saddle, and it's a strip of shallow water that's often found connecting a couple of islands, or perhaps an island with the main shoreline. If the saddle represents a fairly abrupt depth change and has some good cover on it, so much the better. Saddles are major fish magnets, yet almost nobody fishes them.

I like to think of saddles as highways for fish. Fish that swim from the shoreline to the island, or between various islands, will usually follow the saddle, using it as a trail of sorts, rather than just head out into open water and hope for the best. By positioning yourself at some point along this underwater highway, you're in a great position to intercept passing fish. Really big fish will do precisely the same thing; like you, they're in the neighborhood to intercept passing fish.

Saddles are particularly great spots when the wind blows across them. Then I'll cast big, noisy, attention-grabbing lures across the front face of the saddle all day, catching a variety of fish eager for an easy feed. The reason wind affects saddles so profoundly is simple: wind makes waves, and waves move stuff like algae. When the wind blows onto a saddle (or a shoal or a shoreline), small fish gobble the stuff up like mad, taking advantage of an easy feeding opportunity. Bigger fish get right in line and stuff themselves on smaller fish that get so caught up in feeding they lose caution. Because the action is so visual and so aggressive, fast-moving, flashy lures get the most strikes. Because you can cover so much water with these lures, and thus put your offering in front of more fish over the course of an afternoon, this is one situation where lures frequently work better than live bait.

Water lily is one of the most abundant freshwater plants. It provides cover for all sorts of fish, from brook trout in the north to largemouth bass in the south.

Fishing the Weeds

Whether you fish a shoreline or an offshore reef, chances are you'll find the most abundant type of cover is some form of aquatic vegetation. Some weeds attract fish, while others don't. So how do you tell good weeds from bad?

All weeds aren't the same, so your fishing approach shouldn't be the same either. To catch fish in the weeds, you need to learn to identify a handful of aquatic plants, because fish holding under lily pads sometimes behave differently from those tucked into a clump of coontail. Each type of weed has its own unique physical properties, too, which can affect the type of lure and presentation you use.

Forget about trying to identify every type of weed that grows in North American lakes and rivers. Instead, focus on learning different weed families rather than individual species. This makes more sense, because it doesn't really matter if you can't tell a sedge from a bulrush; you fish them both the same way. From a fishing point of view we can group common freshwater weeds into four basic groups, which I call pads, grasses, cabbage, and bushes. These are arbitrary names, but they do the job from an angler's point of view.

Pads

Lily pads, that is. It is pretty well impossible to mistake a water lily for anything else. There are more than a dozen species, all of which grow in shallow water with a soft bottom. Look for a clump of round green disks floating on the surface in shallow water and you've found lily pads.

Lily pads attract fish for many reasons. The shade they provide gives shelter from the hot sun. I've read that the water temperature under a thick pad bed can be as much as ten degrees Fahrenheit (6°C) cooler than open areas exposed to direct sunlight. This is a huge difference for a fish. Lily pads also provide fish an opportunity to ambush surface prey like frogs, snakes, and salamanders.

Most lily pad fishing is for largemouth bass, panfish, and northern pike, but muskie, walleye, and even brook trout will use pads at various times of the year. Pad fishing is a highly visual game, whether you're fishing on the surface or somewhere beneath it.

The simplest approach is to work a highly visible, weedless surface bait that you can cover a bit of water with, like a Heddon Moss Boss, retrieved right through the pads, occasionally dropping it down into the holes. Fish generally plaster these lures, so it's an intensely exciting way to fish. The hotter and sunnier the weather, the more likely this style of fishing will pay off. The reason is simple: hot, sunny weather drives more fish under the shade of the pads. More fish in a small area makes them highly competitive. When something small moves by, fish will often grab it immediately, if only so the other fish don't get it first.

The slow route to pad fishing is to flip a plastic worm, or perhaps a jig, along the edge of the pads, working all the nooks, crannies and open spots. This works better when conditions aren't ideal. If there's a wind blowing, fish the windward side of the pads this way and you can really do well.

The third option in pad fishing is to very slowly work a Texas-rigged plastic worm right through the thick stuff. This is slow fishing that takes a certain amount of patience but catches a lot of very big fish.

The fourth method of pad fishing, and one that I like very much, is to use a small float and a live bait, cast along the edge of the pads or into any holes and openings in the cover. This is by far the best way to catch bragging-sized panfish like bluegill, pumpkinseed, and crappie, as well as bragging-sized brook trout in cold-water lakes.

Grasses

I consider grasses to include any type of stalk-like weed without branches, that looks like the grass on my lawn. I fish three different kinds of grasses, starting with bulrush.

A lot of people refer to bulrushes as pencil weeds or reeds. Bulrush grows on hard bottoms, usually sand, in water as deep as six or seven feet.

Although you usually see only the tips poking out of the water, bulrush can extend as much as six feet above the surface.

Bulrush is a breeze to fish. To work it quickly, try throwing a spinnerbait, weedless spoon, or buzzbait, casting across the clump and retrieving it right through the middle. Fish carefully any openings, holes, or paths through the bulrush. As always, the side facing the wind or the side offering the most shade is your best bet. For a slower approach you can try working small crankbaits through it if the cover's not too thick. Don't laugh—working shallow-running crankbaits through the grass is a smart technique that has won a lot of big tournaments.

Soft plastic jerkbaits like the Slug-Go are always a good bet for fishing open-water grasses like bulrush, as are topwater plugs you can work through the openings. Grasses are a lot like pads in that your approach is extremely visual. You can fish quickly and rely on getting reflex strikes. Fish can see a long way through the stalks and navigate easily between the weeds, so you can attract their attention from a surprising distance.

Some anglers confuse bulrush with cattail, which is another type of grass that's important to anglers. Cattail grows in extremely dense clumps usually right on the shoreline, and is commonly seen rimming shallow, marshy bays. It's found on softer bottoms than bulrush. Cattail attracts pike and largemouth bass in the spring and summer. Both will often burrow right under the edge of the plant, so flipping a plastic worm, or a weedless jig, along a cattail bank is often the best approach. This is slower fishing than working bulrushes, but still a matter of drawing a strike based on reflex. You drop the worm into the holes, and if the fish is there, it will usually hit right away. It doesn't take long to work a cattail bank this way.

In the fall, cattail attracts walleye. The best fishing is at night, twitching floating minnowbaits along the edge of the weeds. If you time your trip to coincide with the annual frog migration, you can hammer big walleye all night long. But even if you miss the frogs returning to the marsh before winter sets in, you can still have a ball as walleye chow down on chub, shiners, and other shallow minnows that patrol the edge of the cover.

The third kind of grass I fish isn't really a grass at all. Called sand grass by anglers, it's a crispy green, spidery plant with small petals growing directly off the main stalk every couple of inches. It has a definite odor that is tough to describe, almost a spicy smell. The stuff grows over firm, sandy bottoms in water as deep as forty feet (12 m). Sand grass grows in thin clumps, and provides ideal cover for crayfish, small minnows, and insects, which in turn makes it a great place to find smallmouth bass, walleye, rainbow trout, brook trout, and pike. Depending on the water depth, jig over it, or try retrieving crankbaits, deep-diving minnowbaits, or slow-rolled spinnerbaits right through the stuff.

Cabbage

Most anglers have heard or read about cabbage being a great place to find all sorts of fish. Yet I'm amazed how few anglers actually fish it. Cabbage, properly called pondweed, belongs to a family with more than fifty different species. Cabbage grows entirely submerged in thick clumps, often as deep as twenty feet (6 m) or more. The leaves are thin and crisp, so when your lure gets caught, you can rip the hooks free with a sharp snap of the wrist. Broadleaf cabbage is probably best known for its reputation as a pike and muskie producer. But largemouth bass, walleye, crappie, and big perch also find it attractive (which is no doubt why the muskie and big pike are there in the first place).

Trolling over cabbage beds is the standard technique for pike and muskie, but casting big jerkbaits, shallow-running crankbaits, and huge spinners and spoons all produce well. For bass and walleye, take the same approach but scale down your lure size, or try dropping a weedless jig into the open holes.

Cabbage has a lot going for it from a fish's point of view. The crispy leaves provide shade and cover, plus enormous amounts of oxygen, even through the heat of summer. In the fall it's one of the last plants to die off, so it holds fish very late in the year. And the fact that it grows in dense stands in deeper water makes it a hit with migratory fish, which may only stop by for a couple of hours at a time.

Because they're bushier than grasses or pads, you have to fish cabbage beds a bit slower and more thoroughly. Early and late in the day you're more likely to find fish sitting up shallow, among the tips of the leaves. By midday they'll often burrow a little deeper into the cover. So, early and late you can cover cabbage beds with faster-moving lures and a horizontal approach, while midday hours are best spent probing the deep holes with vertical approaches using jigs and plastic worms.

Narrow-leaf and round-leaf cabbages are also good fish producers, but due to the fact that they provide less shade, fish will often hold deeper and tighter to the bases of these plants. That's particularly true with walleye. It makes these cabbages a little more difficult to fish than the broadleaf types.

Narrow-leaf cabbage is spinnerbait country. Few other lures allow you to work as deep and slow without getting fouled in the cover. Instead of working the tops of the plants, work a few feet deeper, bouncing bottom now and then. Weedless jigs also work well in narrow-leaf cabbage, especially on bright days when fish will often bury themselves among the roots.

Bushes

I use the term *bushes* to cover all weeds that grow in enormous, thick, tangled gobs, which can be murder to fish properly. There are dozens of plants that fall into this category, but the two best known are milfoil and coontail.

Milfoil is a very common plant that grows as deep as thirty feet (9 m). Look for a dense forest of individual single-stalk plants, each with hundreds of short, narrow, dark green petals or leaves stretching along its entire length, and you've found milfoil. There are several different species, but without a biology degree, forget about trying to tell them apart.

Milfoil attracts bass, pike, walleye, and muskie, but not in the same numbers as cabbage. Being a thinner plant, it doesn't afford the same level of cover as cabbage, for either game fish or prey species. Fish it with a spinnerbait or weedless spoon, or by tossing a topwater plug or buzzbait overtop. Milfoil is a fibrous plant, particularly the main stalk, so once you get your hooks fouled in it, the plant will cling to the lure like it was glued there. Be prepared to reel in a lot of weeds when you fish milfoil, even when using supposedly "weedless" lures.

Coontail is even worse in this regard. Hook a strand of coontail and your lure turns into a six-foot-long green rope. Coontail looks exactly as its name implies—a bushy green raccoon tail. Coontail grows entirely submerged and can live in water as deep as 30 feet (9 m) or more. It doesn't take root but grows in huge clumps as thick as 10 feet (3 m) that just lie on the bottom. Hook a chunk of coontail and the soft plant will wrap around the hook. It's not crispy like cabbage, so no amount of wrist-snapping will free it. You get a green blob at the end of your line, as well as the fun job of peeling it all away from your bait once you've reeled it in.

Having said all that, coontail is a marvelous plant to fish, for it really attracts fish, walleye in particular. Coontail is also a good bass and pike producer, but like milfoil, it is slow to fish. This makes it a particularly good bet on lakes and rivers that get a lot of fishing pressure. Most anglers will fish the easy stuff like pads and grasses, ignoring the tougher cover. Sometimes the fish in coontail and milfoil haven't seen a lure in months, so they can be much easier to catch—provided you can get at them.

Using Maps to Find Fishing Spots

I've become a real fan of using maps to find my fishing spots, since I can eyeball the entire lake at once and immediately see how one shoreline compares with another. I break the shoreline into sections and prioritize which ones seem to have the best structure. A chunk of shore where you have a long point, a vast bay, and an inflowing creek all together in close proximity holds far more promise than a straight, uniform, featureless stretch. I then look for offshore spots like reefs, shoals, and saddles. Scanning a map this way, before even leaving the dock, allows me to eliminate a lot of unproductive water right from the get-go, and to spend my time concentrating on the spots that have the best fish-attracting features.

Navigation charts are tremendous aids in locating great fishing spots located off the shorelines. Essentially a map of the lake bed, they reveal drop-offs, reefs, shoals, saddles, and all sorts of other features that attract fish. Used in conjunction with a good depth finder, they can put you on fish that other anglers ignore.

I use two types of maps. Topographic maps offer a detailed view of the land features surrounding the lake. Topo maps reveal things like rapid changes in elevation. Since what happens on land usually continues the same way underwater, they can reveal the location of underwater drop-offs. Topographic maps also reveal features like marshes and inflowing streams.

While a topo map can be helpful in pinpointing shoreline hot spots, a good navigation chart can be worth its weight in diamonds when it comes to finding offshore spots that are hidden from sight. Most navigable waterways have been plotted by the U.S. or Canadian federal government and are available as hydrographic charts, commonly called navigational charts. Most marine stores and many fishing stores sell them. Charts are like a topographic map of the lake bed, revealing depths, depth contours, shoals, reefs, saddles, channels, and more. Some even show the location of major weedbeds or of wrecks. Used in conjunction with a depth finder and perhaps a GPS unit, they're invaluable to an angler. It's as close as you can get to actually draining the lake and taking a look at what's down there.

Daily and Seasonal Considerations

Over time you'll come to notice that some fishing spots produce well only at a certain time of day or during a particular season. You will find spots that seem to be best in the morning, and discover that places that were crawling with fish in May seem pretty barren in August. All fishing spots are subject to daily and seasonal influences.

Daily influences affect fish the same way they affect people. Fish are not active twenty-four hours a day, and it would be unreasonable to expect otherwise. Just as you and I have some times of day when we're more or less energetic, so it is with fish. This is where knowing a thing or two about the fish you're trying to catch becomes important. Because different types of fish react to environmental conditions in different ways, they're not all active at the same time. Walleye, for instance, have unusual eye structures that allow them exceptional vision in dim light. While prey species like perch and shiners have a tough time seeing anything early and late in the day, walleye can see just perfectly in the dim light. So, as you would expect, that's precisely when walleye hunt—because that's when they enjoy an advantage over their prey. Largemouth bass, on the other hand, are a species that truly enjoys warmth. A bright, sunny afternoon that would send walleye scurrying for cover suits largemouth to a T. So they're active when the walleye are not.

Daily activity levels of fish are linked to seasonal influences. Remember that fish are cold-blooded animals, and as such, their activity is to a large degree controlled by water temperature. A spot that's great in the afternoons in the spring may be a bust in the afternoons in the summer.

For example, northern pike are what biologists call a cool-water species; they don't like things too hot, nor do they like things too cold. In the spring, right after pike spawn, it's common to find them foraging in shallow bays. The best fishing always comes in the afternoon, after the sun has warmed the shallow water for several hours. Fish those shallow bays early in the day and you'll probably have poor fishing. Go back in mid-afternoon and it's a whole different ball game. With a couple of hours of sunshine to warm the shallows, big pike move in and feed aggressively.

Yet go back to the same spot in August and guess what? You won't find many big pike at any time of day, regardless of how much sunshine you get. This is because, even early in the day, those spots are just too warm for a big pike's comfort. Come autumn, however, the big fish return, as water temperatures in the fertile shallows are again at a level that pike can tolerate. And that daily pattern of sedentary mornings and active afternoons is repeated.

This combination of daily and seasonal influences applies to all species of fish, and it's something to think about when you're searching for a fishing spot. Finding a place with a good combination of structure and cover is one thing—but are you there at the right time?

CHAPTER 3

Fishing with Live Bait

Worms

The most basic approach to fishing is the Huck Finn style: sit on the end of a dock with a cane pole, a short length of line, a small hook, and a worm. That's how I started fishing three decades ago and it remains a highly effective approach. The key to it all is the worm.

Why fish eat worms is anyone's guess. It's not as if worms are a regular part of their diet. Fish don't normally climb out onto land and burrow through the earth after them, just as worms don't make a habit of swimming in lakes. Yet worms still catch fish like magic. Something about them just screams *food*, and fish universally respond. I have caught a huge variety of fish species on worms: largemouth bass, smallmouth bass, walleye, panfish, pike, muskie, several species of trout, catfish, carp, even salmon. I've never tried, but I suspect they would work pretty well in the ocean too, for a variety of saltwater species. I've even used them for ice fishing, when every worm in nature lay buried under two feet of snow.

Worms make a wonderful bait from an angler's perspective too. They're relatively easy to care for, they come packaged in these neat little Styrofoam tubs, and it seems like every gas station outside the city limits sells them for a few bucks a dozen. Talk about convenience.

The worms that we buy from gas stations and bait shops are harvested by commercial worm pickers, who often arrange lease deals with golf courses and farms for rights to the worms. It's quite an industry, and it's wildly competitive. A good commercial picker can harvest up to four thousand worms a night. It's back-breaking work, but a quick-handed picker can make a good buck. Worms are then piled into big flat containers and trucked off to a warehouse, where they're counted and split into smaller containers. Most bait stores will buy them by the skid, sorting them into packages of one or two dozen. A big bait store can go through a million worms a year. I know of one tackle shop in Toronto that, year after year, sells an average of forty thousand worms on the opening weekend of walleye season alone.

Canadian worm brokers ship truckloads of worms, which they sell as "Canadian nightcrawlers," to clients in the United States through the summer. Each day from April through October, dozens of eighteen-wheel refrigerated semis, fully loaded with worms, cross the international border. By the end of the year we're talking about enough worms to completely fill a medium-sized stadium. Even at wholesale prices, this is big business.

What's most interesting is that all of the better anglers I know still go out and pick their own. There are certain advantages to "growing your own," as it's called, cost being the least of it. The easiest way to gather your own worms for fishing is to go out on a warm, rainy evening with a flashlight and simply pick them up off the sidewalk. If you're in a productive area

Most anglers begin by fishing with worms, and why not? When they produce fish like Bob Bailey's beautiful walleye, it's hard to argue their effectiveness.

it's possible to gather a couple of hundred worms this way in a very short time, which should keep you in bait for months. Toss any that appear sick or injured, and keep only the ones that seem lively and healthy. For what it's worth, the thick brown end is the head, the thin pale end is the tail, and the thick, fleshy, smooth part about midway down the body is called the collar.

You store worms in a proper worm container, which you can buy at just about any tackle store. Resembling a small flat cooler, worm bins are made of a compressed fiber that breathes, allowing air circulation. Rather than fill it with dirt, you mix up a commercially sold worm bedding that's far cleaner to handle. You then feed the worms store-bought powdered worm food. Once you're done feeding them, the worm bin goes into the bottom of the refrigerator.

Commercial worm containers stored in a refrigerator will keep night crawlers happy for months, providing you're careful about keeping the bedding damp and you feed them according to the directions on the worm food package. In a short time the worms develop a thick, glossy skin, appear to be stronger and healthier, and look like incredibly happy, healthy worms that no fish could pass up. After all, good worm fishing demands good worms! Skinny worms, sleepy worms, and worms that appear limp and lifeless just won't cut it. For really hot fishing you need

thick, juicy, athletic worms that look like they've spent some serious time in the gym. They also stay on the hook far better than their store-bought cousins, and I'm convinced they catch more fish.

Regardless of whether you gather them yourself or buy them from a store, the trick to fishing with worms is to try and keep your tackle as simple as possible. The idea is to create the appearance that this delicious worm somehow tumbled into the water all on its own. That means using a small, thin wire hook, a light line, and as little weight as you can get away with. There is no need for a steel leader, snaps, swivels, or any other additional tackle. Keep it simple.

You hook the worm once and once only, either through the nose or through the collar. Unless bait-stealing panfish are a real problem, don't repeatedly

The trick with worms is to use small, fine wire hooks and impale them once only, through either the nose or the collar. That way the worm can wriggle enticingly.

impale the worm so it becomes a squishy ball on your hook. Not only does this look decidedly unnatural, but it will kill the worm in short order. A worm hooked just once through the nose or collar can stretch and writhe and wriggle enticingly, while one that's balled on the hook can't do anything but sit there like a hunk of liver. Remember, a fresh, lively bait is what works best.

Don't worry about a fish having a difficult time getting the whole worm in its mouth. Even rather small fish are more than capable of fully ingesting a six-inch (15 cm) worm in one swift bite. If you don't believe me, drop one or two worms into the water off the end of any dock, and watch as small perch and sunfish gobble them down effortlessly. Most fish can eat a prey item that's up to about 25 percent of their own size, so even a python-sized worm isn't much of a problem for the average bass, walleye, or trout.

Great worm fishing demands great worms! Perhaps a specialized worm box, worm bedding and worm food sounds like we're going a little overboard, but a little preparation makes for a far more effective bait.

Worms need to be kept cool. As I mentioned earlier, the best place to store them long-term is in a refrigerator, although that doesn't go over well in every household. I have some acquaintances who purchased bar fridges for storing worms, and this seems to work well while keeping other family members happy. If the fridge is out of bounds for worms, then a cool and shaded basement corner will do for shorter-term storage.

While out fishing, carry your worm tubs in a small cooler that's partially filled with ice. If you're wading, you can get little plastic boxes with flip-top lids that attach to a belt. They're okay for a few hours, but on a warm, sunny day your worms won't last longer than that. I've found that periodically dripping a handful of

cold water into the bedding helps extend their life, but be careful not to saturate them. Those little boxes don't have any drainage, so it doesn't take much to leave your worms swimming in muddy water.

Minnows

Next to worms, minnows are the most popular bait used by anglers. As most types of predatory fish survive by eating smaller fish, minnows are a terrific choice as a bait. Sold by the dozen in marinas and bait stores everywhere, they're almost as convenient as worms to obtain and use.

The word *minnow* is the proper name for an entire family of fish, but from an angler's perspective it also refers to smaller members of the perch, whitefish, and sucker families. The most common types of minnows sold as baitfish include golden and emerald shiners, creek chubs, dace, and various types of suckers. It is not uncommon to find that one variety of minnow works better than another in certain locations, due to natural availability of one species over the other. For example, the lakes near my home teem with emerald shiners. Because most fish in those lakes are accus-

Minnows are the hands-down favorite for many anglers, especially when fishing in cooler temperatures. Minnows stay lively in cold water, where worms or leeches go limp.

tomed to eating them, emerald shiners tend to out-produce other types of minnows as bait. This is why I always try to buy my minnows as close to my fishing location as possible; chances are they were trapped locally, and are of a species and size range that game fish in that area are accustomed to eating.

Minnows for fish bait range considerably in size, based upon what it is you're trying to catch. Minnows sold for perch, crappie, white bass, and other small-mouthed fish are typically from one to two inches (2.5–5 cm) in length, whereas those bought by anglers in quest of bass, walleye, and trout might be twice that size. The biggest baits—suckers in the twelve-inch (30 cm) range and up—are bought by anglers targeting pike, muskie, sturgeon, and giant catfish.

The simplest way to store minnows while fishing is in a minnow bucket. These affairs look like a plastic pail with a french-fry basket inside; when you lift the basket portion, the water drains out, leaving the minnows flopping on the bottom so you can easily grab one and not even get your hands wet. Other styles of minnow bucket have floats on the sides and small holes in the bottom and sides, so that the water within the bucket can circulate and refresh. You simply tie the bucket to a short rope and let it float in the water.

There are numerous ways to hook minnows, and this can be the

Leeches are exceptional baits for a variety of freshwater fish, and walleye and smallmouth bass in particular.

subject of considerable debate among anglers. The most common technique is to impale the minnow through both lips, which leaves it free to swim around as it likes. Given that most predatory fish eat their lunch headfirst, this method also provides a high percentage of successful hookups. Other anglers prefer to hook the minnow through the base of the dorsal (back) or anal (you know where) fin. By positioning the hook closer to the center of the body, the theory is that fewer bites will be missed. Other anglers believe that a minnow so hooked has a more erratic swimming action in the water. I tend to believe that any minnow hooked in any way will swim erratically, so I don't know if there's a great deal of validity to that argument.

As when fishing with worms, it pays to use smaller hooks of thin wire and with fine barbs when fishing with minnows, as they tend to do less damage to the bait. Minnows are rather fragile to begin with, and will fly off the hook if you're not careful when casting. The thin hook helps keep them where they need to be.

In some areas there are regulations against the use of live minnows, so it should be noted that dead minnows work almost as well, particularly if you can give them a bit of life by continually twitching the tip of your fishing rod. Dead minnows can be hooked straight through the body, as there's no worry about making them any more dead than they already are.

While minnows work well year-round, they're particularly good baits when you're fishing early or late in the season and the water is cold—50°F (10°C) or less. Minnows out-produce other baits then because they remain active. In the chill water most other live baits become limp and lifeless, where minnows keep right on swimming. This is why they're the hands-down choice of ice fishermen everywhere.

Leeches

No, I'm not talking about the notorious bloodsuckers found in so many cheesy late-night horror movies. The leeches used as baits are ribbon leeches, harmless vegetarian creatures that are abundant in many lakes and rivers across North America. Leeches are an exceptional bait for a variety of fish, including both largemouth and smallmouth bass, walleye, yellow perch, black crappie, most kinds of trout, and even pike and muskie. You have only to see one swim in the water to understand why fish eat them. I have no doubt that to a fish, a leech looks every bit as good as a succulent roast turkey does to a hungry person.

In your hand a leech looks a bit like a slab of liver. The pointy end is the tail, the duller end the head. The little sticky spot on the head is a suction disk, where it will attach itself to plants—or your finger. Because a wet leech is about as slippery as a wet ice cube, they're tough to handle when you're trying to put one on a hook. I always carry a small towel in my tackle bag and have found that drying the leech solves the problem in a hurry. When you can get a grip on a leech, you can easily hook it once through the suction disk, where it will stay on the hook for a long time with minimal damage.

Leeches are about as slippery as a wet ice cube. Drying them off on an old towel makes it far easier to put them on the hook.

Bait stores sell leeches in water-filled Styrofoam tubs similar to the ones used for worms, basically a squat soup bowl with a clear plastic lid. Leeches are extremely sensitive to heat and sunlight, so be sure to keep them cool and shaded in the boat or they'll die in no time flat. Ideally, you should carry them like worms, in a small cooler partially filled with ice. When you need a new bait, just pull out the tub, and put it back in the cooler when you're done.

Crayfish

North American lakes and rivers are home to several different species of crayfish, which are preyed upon by virtually everything else that swims. When you consider how much people like eating lobster, you can only imagine how popular these little freshwater crustaceans are with most types of game fish.

Crayfish are found in rocky areas, where they feed on vegetation, detritus, and other bottom matter, scooting around backwards from one hiding place to the next as quickly as possible to avoid detection. Most bait dealers trap crayfish from fertile lakes, streams, and even ponds. Ranging in length from an inch and a bit (2.5 cm) to about three and a half inches (9 cm), they're perfect baits for many types of fish, but are especially popular among smallmouth bass anglers. In some places crayfish can represent up to 80 percent of a smallmouth's diet, so no wonder they're so effective.

If you can find them, soft-shelled crayfish, which are crayfish in the process of shedding their shell, are the best baits going. When a crayfish outgrows its tough outer shell, it sheds it and a new shell takes its place. After they shed their old external shell, crayfish are extremely vulnerable while waiting for the new one to harden, a process that can take two or three days. If you should ever be lucky enough to find soft-shelled crayfish, buy every one you can and get ready for a busy day on the water.

The best way to fish with crayfish is to hook them once through the tail with a thin wire hook, and fish them on the bottom in the type of rocky areas where they're naturally found. You may have to give your bait a little lift every now and then, because it will continually try to hide under the rocks, but it shouldn't take long to attract attention from passing fish. Along the edge of weedbeds is another prime place to fish with crayfish.

Like leeches and worms, crayfish are normally sold in little Styrofoam tubs, which work fine for short-term storage. As always, keep them cool, ideally on ice in a little cooler. Crayfish also do well in a minnow bucket providing the water's not too warm.

If you have some crayfish left over at the end of the day, you can keep them in the refrigerator in a small container of water. Make sure you have a secure lid, however, as they can—and will—climb out of anything left unsecured, a little gem of knowledge I learned the hard way. I have a sixty-five-gallon (250 L) aquarium at home, and I once got the brilliant idea of keeping several leftover crayfish in the big tank between fishing trips. To my utter disbelief, every single one of them somehow managed to climb out of the tank within a day and a half. So long as I live I shall never forget the blood-curdling scream of my now ex-wife when she discovered one of them marching across the bathroom floor. Let's just say that caused a wee bit of a stir, and leave it at that.

It is also important to keep an eye on crayfish for another reason: nothing smells as bad as a dead crayfish (yet another little gem of knowledge, learned in the days following the mass escape from the fish tank). If they don't look like they're going to make it till your next fishing trip, release them or flush them down the toilet, because the odor of a decomposing crayfish will cross your eyes like nothing else on this planet.

Insects

Insects form a substantial part of the diet of many kinds of fish. Anglers regularly use two different types: crickets and grasshoppers.

Crickets, sold in most pet stores as food for lizards and snakes, make wonderful baits, particularly for trout in small to medium-sized streams. Hooked once through the body and drifted through a deep, shady pool on a small hook and thin-diameter line, crickets fool even the wariest trout. Although crickets are a pain in the neck to extract from the container (normally a paper bag) and hold on a hook, they catch trout like magic. I once saw a device that looked somewhat like a turkey baster, used to dispense crickets one at a time into your hand. I should have bought the silly thing when I had the chance, for I've never seen another. Crickets are also tremendous baits for panfish like bluegill, pumpkinseed, and yellow perch. Dropped into the shade of an old boathouse, they're almost unbeatable when panfish are your target species.

Grasshoppers can also be magnificent baits, but they work only for a short period of time each year, in late summer when huge numbers of these creatures wind up in the water along lakeshores and where streams flow through grassy fields. In the right place and at the right time, however, they can be awesome baits. In fact, grasshoppers are probably *the* late-summer bait for trophy stream trout, particularly in western Canada and the western United States. All it takes is a good stiff wind to blow hundreds of these creatures into streams, where the trout immediately gobble them up. I've watched huge brown trout—some approaching thirty inches (76 cm) in length—slashing through water only inches deep where high grass ran along the edge of the creek, hammering grasshoppers as soon as they hit the water. Think any of those fish would even look at one of my artificial flies? Not a chance—they wanted the real thing and nothing else.

Caterpillars also have their days as bait. One of the biggest stream-resident brown trout I've ever seen came on a sunny spring afternoon from a small wooded brook about two hours from my home, on a little green caterpillar plucked from the side of a tree. I should note that the fish was caught not by me but by someone else after I had fished the pool unsuccessfully for more than half an hour. I had given up and was sitting on the bank eating a sandwich when another angler approached and began fishing. When he too drew a blank, he rummaged around on the shoreline, found the caterpillar—and the rest, as they say, is history.

The great thing about using grasshoppers and caterpillars for bait is that you don't have to worry about caring for them at all. However, when you need a new bait, you're back up on the bank scrounging, and that does cut into one's fishing time.

If you really want to get sneaky on stream trout or wise old smallmouth bass that prowl rocky shorelines, try flipping over a couple of submerged rocks plucked from the bottom and see what you find underneath. In a fertile lake or river, chances are you'll discover a variety of little dragon-like creatures scurrying around on the bottom surface of the rock. These are the larvae of various types of aquatic insects, and are collectively called nymphs. Some of the larger ones, such as the hellgrammite (the larva of a Dobson fly), are almost as big as a cricket, while others are so tiny they're almost impossible to put on a hook. But if you're patient, you should be able to collect enough of the little beasties to keep you in bait all day. Fished on a very tiny hook tied to thin, clear monofilament line, live nymphs are exceptional baits that few anglers bother with. I almost never bother with them myself, truth be known; but if the fish refuse everything else, a live nymph will sometimes produce results.

Frogs

Let me state categorically right from the beginning: I don't like using frogs for bait. In fact, I really *don't* use frogs as bait. But this is a fishing book, and since we're talking about live baits in this chapter, we have to talk about frogs, because nothing on earth is as effective when it comes to catching bass, muskie, and pike.

I remember vacationing with my family, when I was about twelve years old, at a rented cottage in south-central Ontario. The cottage overlooked a small lake that held good numbers of very nice smallmouth bass. I had been having a ball, catching an assortment of panfish and numerous plump smallmouth up to about two and a half pounds (1.1 kg) by casting from the shoreline in front of the cottage, when one morning I heard an enormous splash and looked out onto the lake to see a massive boil on the surface. I didn't actually see the fish that made the commotion, but by the volume of water it was moving, it had to be a monster. Evidently my father had been reading my mind because at that moment he stepped over beside me and asked if I knew where I could find any frogs. There was a marshy creek a short hike down the road from the cottage, and I had seen many frogs there, I told him. With that, he handed me a big white bucket and directed me to go catch three or four medium-sized leopard frogs.

The little creek was alive with amphibians, so it didn't take very long before I had caught a half-dozen and returned to the cottage. We put them in a floating minnow pail, which was tied to the end of the dock. At my father's urging I tied a number-four hook to my line and impaled one of the frogs lightly through the lips. With a delicate cast I lobbed it out into the lake, as close as I could get to where the giant fish had jumped earlier. For a brief moment the frog floated still on the glassy-calm lake surface, the ripples from its landing fading away in concentric circles.

Before I could say a word, there was a boil on the surface the size of a car, and the frog was gone. For a moment I felt a tremendous surge on my fishing rod, then everything went quiet and my line lay limp in the water. I reeled in, saw that the end of my line was cut so cleanly I couldn't have done a better job with a fillet knife, and my father calmly announced, "Muskie."

The next morning, a twelve-inch (30 cm) wire leader separated the hook from my line. Again I hooked one of the leopard frogs through the lips, and again I lobbed it out into the lake. Again it sat quietly on the surface of the glassy-calm lake for a few moments. Then it kicked its legs once and disappeared. A few moments later I beached a four-pound (1.8 kg) smallmouth bass—by far the biggest smallmouth I had ever seen. It wasn't the muskie I had envisioned, but I wasn't complaining one bit.

Frogs can be a tremendous bait for walleye, particularly in the fall when frogs migrate to deeper water in marshes, where they hibernate in the bottom mud. Where I live in the Great Lakes region, this event usually coincides with the first full moon in October. On a clear night, walleye absolutely gorge themselves on frogs, darting through the shallows with complete abandon. I've only hit it right a couple of times, but when I did, it was some of the easiest walleye fishing I've ever experienced.

From the average person's perspective, a frog is a frog is a frog. But not so for anglers. When you're looking for bait, leopard frogs are the critters of choice. These medium-sized frogs are brilliant green in color and have numerous round, dark spots on the back. They also have a ridge on each side of their back, extending from their eyes to their butt. Leopard frogs are among the most common frogs in North America, and are abundant in marshy bays and creeks, and even on wet lawns. The closely related pickerel frog, which has square-shaped dark blotches on its green body, also catches fish but never seems to produce as well as a leopard frog; I don't pretend to know why. Bullfrogs and green frogs, identifiable by their huge eardrums and lack of spotting or ridges on the back, also work, but only muskie, pike, and the biggest bass are big enough to handle them.

I have come to prefer using imitation frogs over real ones, as they're far less expensive and, truth to tell, I've just never been comfortable using amphibians for bait. But as live baits go, there can be no denying: for big fish, frogs are one of the best.

CHAPTER 4

Hooks, Lines, and Sinkers

Fish Hooks

The most basic piece of fishing tackle in the world is also one of the most highly evolved. Of course I'm talking about the plain old fish hook. Modern fish hooks are remarkable contraptions. Mass-produced to exacting tolerances yet still retailing for a couple of cents apiece, they're masterpieces of design. Hooks come in thousands of styles and sizes, ranging from diminutive versions as small as a grain of rice, designed for competitive match fishing, to enormous shark hooks as big as a toaster. Hooks are truly remarkable creations—and so they should be, considering their long and colorful history.

By most accounts fish hooks first appeared on earth more than twenty

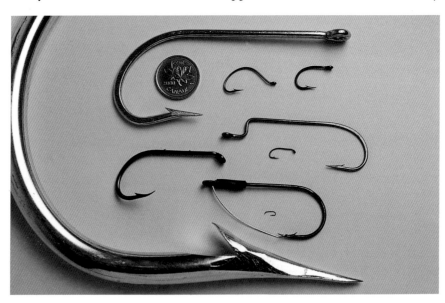

Shown with a penny for comparison, it's easy to see how widely hooks can vary in size.

thousand years ago. The first hooks were made from splintered bones. Rather than impale the fish in the modern manner, these primitive hooks usually acted as a gorge. Once the fish had swallowed the bait, the hook would wedge in its throat. Sort of like swallowing a miniature umbrella, it would go in easily but open up when the swallower tried to back it out. Our primitive cave angler would then haul the fish up the bank and unceremoniously whack it on the head with a rock. (Remember, catch and release was not as popular twenty thousand years ago as it is today.) The cave angler would then go home and lie like hell about the one that got away.

The first primitive copper hooks are believed to have made their appearance about seven thousand years ago, and have been documented in descriptions of artificial flies dated to 2,000 B.C. Mass-produced steel hooks surfaced with the Industrial Revolution and have been going strong ever since.

Hook sizes are measured numerically. For freshwater fishing in North America the range most commonly used would stretch from a tiny size 16, barely large enough to impale a pea, to a big size 6/0, substantial enough to handle a foot-long baitfish. Hook sizes 16, 14, 12, and 10 are generally used in fishing for small-mouthed species like trout or panfish, using tiny baits like salmon eggs, caterpillars, garden worms, grasshoppers, and the like. Larger size 8, 6, 4, 2, and 1 hooks are more widely used with bass, walleye, salmon, and smaller pike, and are perfect for the most commonly used live baits: dew worms, leeches, frogs, crayfish, and minnows up to about four inches (10 cm) in length. The bigger hooks—sizes 1/0 (pronounced *one-ott*), 2/0, 4/0, 5/0, and 6/0—are most often used when fishing with substantial live baits, or when using bulky soft plastic lures for largemouth bass, pike, and muskie.

The looped end of the hook to which you tie your line is called the eye, and there are three different eye styles that you may encounter. The original fish hooks used a ringed eye, meaning the wire is formed into a straight ring. When fly fishing became popular in the seventeenth century, some manufacturers began bending the eye downwards, to provide greater clearance around the feather dressing, creating what became known as a TDE (turned-down-eye) hook. With the subsequent creation of very small hooks for tiny midge flies, the eye was turned upwards to allow more clearance for the hook point, giving rise to the TUE (turned-up-eye). Whether the hook eye is straight, turned up, or turned down doesn't matter at all to the fish, and has no bearing on hooking efficiency. Straight-ringed eyes are most often seen on cheap hooks, simply because they represent one less step in the manufacturing process.

The straight part of the hook, called the shank, can vary a lot in length. Extra-long shanks are helpful when fishing for species like sunfish, which have small mouths and tend to gobble bait. The extra length simply

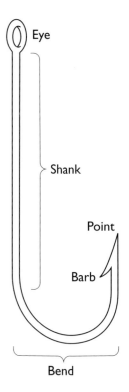

Principle parts of a fish hook: the eye, shank, bend, barb and point.

57

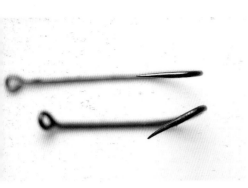

Viewed from below, it's easy to see the difference between a regular hook (top) and an offset hook. Offsetting increases hooking efficiency.

makes it easier to unhook your catch. Extra-short shanks are also available, and are often used when fishing with small baits, such as a single salmon egg. For general-purpose angling, though, hooks of standard shank length work just fine.

The bend of a hook has some bearing on its function. The strongest hooks feature an even round bend; sharp turns in the wire can result in weak spots.

The barb is an obvious feature of any hook, as is the point. They form the business end of the hook, and this is where you will see the difference between a good hook and a cheapie. Quality hooks feature small barbs and fine, machine- or chemically sharpened points. Cheap hooks are simply cut at a sharp angle, resulting in a crude point that will bend easily under pressure. In my view, cheap hooks represent false economy. Of all the expenses you will incur in a day's fishing, hooks must surely rank at the bottom of the list. The small extra cost of premium hooks will result in you catching more fish. It's a worthwhile upgrade.

If you look closely at the sides of some hooks, you will notice that the metal is flattened rather than round, as it is on the shank. Those flattened sides are the mark of a forged hook. Forging greatly increases strength, and is a big plus for heavy-duty situations like fishing for trophy pike, muskie, salmon, or lake trout. You may also notice that some hooks have their point in line with the shank while others have the point bent out a bit to one side. The bent variety, which is called an offset hook, tends to hook fish more efficiently than the straight style and is preferred, especially when using small single hooks with live baits. The trade-off, however, is in cost, as bending the wire out represents another manufacturing expense.

While most hooks have a little barb located just above the point, it is possible to buy barbless hooks. Designed to do less damage to the fish and make the job of unhooking it easier, barbless hooks have been used by some fly fishermen for years, and have begun to catch on among bait and lure anglers as well. Across North America there are more and more places where barbless regulations now apply, including the entire province of Manitoba.

The biggest benefit of barbless hooks seems to come when you hook yourself. On more than one remote northern fly-in trip I've been happy in hindsight about using barbless hooks after removing a large one from some part of my anatomy. When the closest hospital is a couple of hundred miles away, I'll put up with losing a few more fish. While writing this book, in fact, I suffered an unfortunate incident when a fishing companion accidentally buried a large Mepps Muskie Killer into the back of my neck on an errant cast. With the barb buried well out of sight, I wound up with a trip to the emergency room and a five-stitch incision for my trouble.

I'm becoming fonder of barbless hooks these days. You can convert existing hooks to barbless simply by mashing the barb down flat with a pair of pliers, something I find myself doing more and more often.

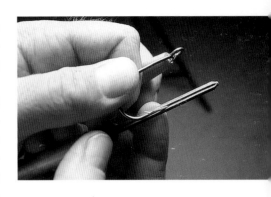

The vast majority of hooks sold for use in fresh water have a bronzed finish, although it is also possible to buy hooks that are chromed or plated with a gold- or red-colored nickel coating. I've always preferred the dull brown, plain Jane bronzed hooks as they're far more subtle than flashy silver or gold ones, which I believe is a plus when dealing with spooky fish. They're also easier on fish. Should you hook a fish very deeply or in a delicate spot, rather than tear more tissue, it's often best simply to cut the line. With the corrosive effect of water and the fish's own enzymes, a bronzed hook will deteriorate and come out of the fish far more quickly than one with a chrome or nickel coating.

One of the most useful accessory items an angler can buy is a small, high quality hook hone. Hooks must be needle sharp to work! Try scratching the point across your thumbnail. If it slides over the nail, it's dull. If it digs in and tries to penetrate, it's sharp enough for use.

About the only other variable in fish hooks is their thickness. All else being equal, a thin hook will penetrate the fish's mouth far more easily than a thicker one. Top-quality hooks use top-grade steel with a very high carbon content, which provides tremendous strength while retaining a fine diameter. These top-grade hooks obviously cost more than hooks made from utility-grade steel. However, I feel it's a worthwhile expense since the hook is the one item of gear that can really make or break your day. If you're going to save money anywhere in your fishing tackle, hooks aren't the place to do so.

Hooks are sold in little bags of ten, or in boxes of fifty or a hundred. I tend to buy them in bulk for, not only is it far less expensive in the long run but also I'm always surprised at how many I go through. I like to carry hooks together in little multi-compartment boxes. My favorite model, which is made by the Plano Molding company, is a double-sided box approximately the size of a cigarette package. Each side of the box has a hinged door with numerous little compartments, so I can store hooks together by size. I find the containers the hooks come in are worthless for storage when they've been opened once or twice, as the little plastic hinge flexes and breaks. The result is hooks all over the place. Arrgghh!

Weights

Most of the fishing done in fresh water occurs below the surface, and over the years anglers have devised an astonishing variety of weights to take their offering down to the fish. Weights, or sinkers, come in almost as wide a range of styles as hooks. The reality, though, is that for freshwater fishing, three or four styles in a narrow range of sizes will handle 99 percent of the situations we're ever likely to find ourselves in.

Split shot sinkers, which look somewhat like little balls with a slot cut in them, are the bread-and-butter sinker for freshwater fishing. Unlike hooks, which are sized by ascending numerical designation, split shot sizing is somewhat puzzling. The smallest size commonly used, at approximately one-sixteenth of an ounce (1.8 g), is size B, followed by BB, 7, 5, 3, and—at almost the size of a fingernail—size 1. Split shot attach easily: just pinch them onto your line with your fingertips, a foot or two up from the hook. If you need more weight, use a larger size or simply attach a second weight.

Split shot can be found in what are termed round and removable styles. Round weights are just what they sound like—a ball with a slit cut through it to accommodate the line. Removable split shot have the little ears attached to the opposite side of the sinker. By pinching the little ears together, you exert a scissors-like action on the weight, opening the slit so the sinker can be removed. For ease of use I quite like the removable variety of split shot and use them almost exclusively. The one situation where I prefer regular round shot is when I'm fishing in areas with strong currents. The theory is that the ears on the removable shot plane in the current and cause the line to spin underwater. I don't know if this is true of not, but I do find I seem to experience fewer tangles if I use the plain round shot when fishing in current, so perhaps there is something to it.

If I find I need a lot of weight, rather than using a number of big split shot, I'll switch to a rubber core sinker instead. Rubber core sinkers are cucumber-shaped lead weights with a hole drilled through from end to end and a slit cut in one side. Running down the center of the sinker, and sticking out the ends, is a core consisting of a soft rubber strip, which gives the sinker its name. To attach one of these to your line you simply slip the fishing line into the open grove, then twist it round the rubber core by pulling on the ends while sliding the line in behind.

Rubber core sinkers are big enough and coarse enough to fill a niche where split shot leave off. For fishing in deep water, where you need to get down there in a hurry, or in a current where the flow will make it necessary to use a lot of weight to reach bottom, they're tough to beat. The great feature of these sinkers is their ease of use. You can remove the sinker as easily as you installed it, with no damage to your line. The rubber core sinkers I generally use range from fingernail-sized to about the size of a small eraser, which might weigh a full two ounces (57 g).

Both split shot and rubber core sinkers are fixed firmly in place on your line. A third style of sinker I always carry with me is nothing more than a clump of lead with a hole drilled in it. It's designed to slide freely up and down the line, and is called a slip sinker. Slip sinkers come in a range of shapes, from little footballs (called egg sinkers) to little bullets (bullet weights) to strange-looking teardrops with a hole in the thin end (walking sinkers). They all work on the same principle of allowing the line to slide freely through the weight. I carry slip sinkers in a range of styles and sizes—mainly the egg- and bullet-shaped ones, ranging from one-eighth to three quarters of an ounce (3.5–21 g).

Slip sinkers are ideal when you're still-fishing with bait for light-biting fish. Ordinarily, when the fish picks up the bait, it will move off in one direction or the other, and soon detect the weight of the sinker on the line. If the fish is shy, it will drop the bait before the angler (that's you) can react. Slip sinkers alleviate this problem. The fish picks up the bait, but because the line can move freely through the weight, the sinker stays on the bottom and the fish feels nothing. Presto! You've got a fish.

What keeps a slip sinker from sliding all the way down the line to tangle with your hook is a stopper of some sort; a small split shot pinched an appropriate distance up the line works well. Other anglers prefer to cut the line a suitable distance up from the hook and tie in a small barrel swivel that's just large enough to not pass through the weight.

The fourth and final type of sinker that I carry is an odd item called a bottom bouncer. These strange-looking contraptions are used exclusively when trolling a lure or bait behind the boat. A bottom bouncer is essentially a clump of weight on a long wire shaft. You tie your line to the wire, then attach your lure or bait on a second length of line from three to five feet (0.9–1.5 m) long. As you troll, the bottom bouncer drags almost plumb below the boat, the wire stem scraping over rocks and logs, keeping the whole works from getting stuck. They're simple but amazingly effective.

Bottom bouncers are typically big sinkers, weighing from ¾ ounce to four ounces (21–113 g) or more. They avoid snags best when fished on as vertical a line as possible, hence the larger weights. You can find them painted in every color of the rainbow, but I sincerely doubt that sinker color makes any difference whatsoever. I buy them in plain unpainted gray and save the extra cash for something else.

Bottom bouncers came into wide use several years ago by tournament walleye anglers, but they have applications everywhere. I've used them for everything from monster walleye to channel catfish, chinook salmon, lake trout, and steelhead. Any time you need to be close to a snaggy bottom, they're tough to beat.

Few materials lend themselves to use as fishing sinkers as well as lead. Not many other materials are as heavy, soft, and inexpensive. Lead, however, is not the nicest stuff to handle, so it is possible to buy fishing sinkers made from a host of alternate materials, including tin, bismuth, brass, and synthetics. Regrettably, none of them work anywhere near as well as lead, and all cost significantly more. So, I stick with lead and think about all the other things in our air, water, and food that will probably kill me first.

Like hooks, sinkers vary somewhat in price. The difference between cheap weights and good weights is usually a matter of a few cents, but it is another worthwhile upgrade in my view. Cheap sinkers are formed with low-grade lead that's often rather stiff and brittle, making the sinker

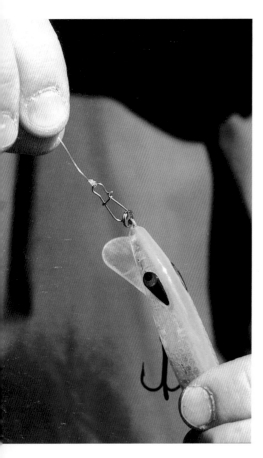

To make lure changes easier, use a small Duolock snap instead of tying your lures directly to the line.

tougher to pinch closed and, especially in the case of split shot, often causing it to nick your line, thus weakening it. Better-quality sinkers use a higher grade of lead that's softer and won't pinch your line. I've used Water Gremlin weights for two decades and have never had a problem. Like hooks, I store them in a small double-sided Plano box for convenience.

Leaders, Snaps, and Swivels

Nothing else in a tackle box seems to be as misunderstood as snaps, swivels, and leaders.

Most of the time, fishing is a less-is-more game; that is, the simpler things are, the better they work. So we tie our fishing line directly to a small hook rather than using another device to secure the hook and line together. If we're fishing with artificial lures, we similarly tie the lure directly to the line with a clean and simple knot. The less stuff we have to deal with, the less fuss we have to contend with, the less likely that something will go wrong, and the fewer components we need to buy.

Nevertheless, there are times when it may not be best to tie directly to your fishing line. The most obvious example would be when fishing for creatures like pike and muskie, which have mouths studded with razor-sharp teeth that will sever fishing line on contact. If we want to hold on to one of these creatures after it bites our lure or bait, we'll need to use something between the hook and line to absorb the punishment from those teeth. That "thing" is a wire leader.

A leader is simply a length of wire from six to thirty-six inches (15–91 cm) long, with a swivel on one end and a snap on the other. Pike and muskie may have sharp teeth, but they're no match for a length of wire. The leader protects our fishing line from being snipped. Personally, I dislike using a leader because I feel it detracts from the attraction of a lure or bait, particularly when fishing with topwaters or soft plastic jerkbaits. But when fishing for pike and muskie, there's simply no alternative: you either use a leader or lose most of the fish you hook.

If I have to use a leader, I pay the money and buy the best ones I can get, which tend to use finer components that nonetheless retain incredible strength. Leaders come in both silver and black finishes. I always buy black because I believe it's less likely to spook a fish. Big fish can take a six-inch (15 cm) leader all the way into their mouth, so I stick with the twelve-inch (30 cm) jobs for casting, and go with the eighteen- or twenty-four-inch (46 or 61 cm) versions for trolling. (I'd use the longer ones all the time if the extra length didn't make casting more difficult.)

I sometimes use leaders when fishing for bass, as they tend to inhabit the same types of places as pike and muskie. I don't need leaders for bass, which have very fine teeth, but I don't like losing expensive bass lures to pike and muskie. In that situation I'll often use fine wire leaders made right on the spot from single-strand stainless steel wire. The wire is very fine and lightweight (sort of like the thinnest string on a guitar), and less prone to affect the action of the smaller bass lures, yet strong enough to save my lures from any greedy pike that happen along.

If bite-offs from pike and muskie aren't going to be a problem but I still want the convenience of using a snap to attach the lure, so I don't have to tie a lot of knots all day, I'll use a simple plain wire snap all by itself. I'll also use snaps when fishing with certain types of lures, like spoons, which can be tough to attach directly to the line on account of their thickness. The best snaps are the Duo-Lock variety, which look like little wire figure eights. Several manufacturers produce Duo-Lock snaps; the better ones are made from stainless steel wire and have an even round bend, giving a fishing lure plenty of freedom of movement. Again, I'll take the black ones over the chrome-plated ones every time, and the smallest I can get away with. Avoid cheap snaps that have sharp bends in the wire, as well as any that use a flat piece of metal to hold the thing closed rather than the intertwined wire of a Duo-Lock; big fish can straighten them out easily.

Swivels are also important with some lures, such as inline spinners or tube jigs, that tend to twist the line. I prefer to use a small black barrel or crane swivel with these baits. Simply cut your line a foot or so up from the lure and tie the swivel in using good knots. It takes care of line twist and keeps the rig looking neat and subtle.

I don't tend to go through a lot of swivels or snaps. Normally, I reserve one compartment in my little hook box for swivels and carry a little container of snaps in my main tackle box, with my lures. Leaders are kept in a long Ziploc-type plastic bag that originally held plastic tie-wraps; this keeps them straight and avoids tangles with other gear.

Floats

Many anglers start out as kids fishing with a worm under a big plastic bobber, and the fact is, that's a great way to catch all kinds of fish. While the cheap, round plastic bobber works, the whole affair becomes much more effective when we substitute a proper wooden float. The difference between a bobber and a float is like the difference between a baggage cart and a BMW. The hard plastic bobbers tend to leak, are prone to crack and break, and are horribly, artificially buoyant, making it difficult for all but the most determined fish to pull them under. More often than not, fish drop the bait when they feel the resistance of the bobber.

Floats, fashioned from balsa wood and shaped like little pencils, teardrops, and such, are another matter altogether. Precision-made, balanced, and naturally buoyant, they betray the take of even gentle biters without alerting the fish that something's wrong with this particular meal. They're ideal for keeping a bait from getting tangled in bottom debris, for keeping one moving along in a slow current, or for presenting an offering to fish that may be suspended in the water column.

I select floats as I do sinkers: a selection of various sizes, some of which fix onto the line, others that can slide freely. Most of the time we want to use floats to present a live bait just above the bottom. Fixed floats, which are generally fixed into position on the line with two pieces of soft rubber tubing, are for fishing in relatively shallow water—basically, as deep as your fishing rod is long. So, you determine the water depth, slide the float an appropriate distance up the line from the hook, attach a couple of weights between the float and the hook to provide casting weight, bait up, and go to it. When the rig hits the water, the sinkers will take the bait down to where the fish are. At that point the float goes from lying on its side to sitting upright. If you've got enough weight on your line, the float should sit vertically with just the tip sticking out of the water. When a fish bites, the float will disappear beneath the surface. You set the hook and the fight's on.

The difficulty with floats comes when you begin fishing in deeper water. Trying to cast a float with five or six feet (1.5 or 1.8 m) of line hanging under it takes a bit of practice; trying to cast one with twenty feet (6 m) of line hanging below is out of the question—and that's where the slip float comes in. Because the line can slide freely through a slip float, we need to use a little stopper of some sort to cock it upright at the correct depth. Most anglers use little neoprene rubber beads that thread onto the line with a little wire device. These beads are small enough to pass through the fishing rod guides and be wound right up onto the reel, yet thick enough to stop the float and make it sit upright when the weights take our bait to the correct depth.

What you do is slide not the float but the little rubber bead up the line the appropriate distance from the hook. If the water is twenty feet (6 m) deep, slide the bead nineteen feet (5.8 m) up the line. Slide on the float, attach a weight a foot or two above the end of the line, and tie on a hook. When you cast, the float will land on its side in the water, the weight will take the bait deep, and line will peel off the reel, slide through the float and follow the weight down into the water. Before long that little rubber bead comes along and, being too thick to pass through the float, plugs the hole. The float pops upright in the water and you're all set. When the float moves, you set the hook, and as you reel in the fish, the float will slide down the line to the weight.

On one occasion some friends and I used slip floats to catch beautiful northern Quebec lake trout that were more than forty feet (12 m) down. Other anglers saw us casting a float with a minnow just two feet (0.6 m)

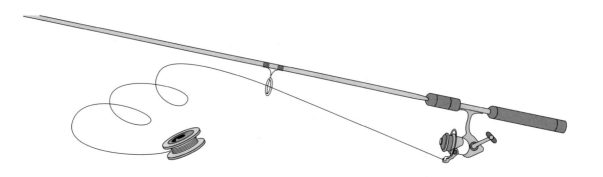

below it and assumed we were hooking the fish just below the surface. Before long, some of them had rigged up with a fixed float two feet (0.6 m) above their hook. They could not understand how it was that we continued to catch fish while they couldn't get a hit. Being basically nice guys, we showed them what we were doing, and after giving them some floats and beads, they soon matched us fish for fish. But without the slip floats there would have been no way any of us could have caught those fish.

On another occasion, while fishing the Gulf coast of Florida, a friend named Mark Kulik and I caught a variety of saltwater game fish, including some black-tipped reef sharks, by fishing live shrimp beneath large slip floats that were designed for freshwater bass and walleye.

I use floats a lot. Apart from the fact that they work so well, I really enjoy the visual aspect of fishing with them. Seeing the brightly colored float plunge beneath the surface stops my heart. It's a feeling of exhilaration that just can't be matched, regardless of whether it's a sunfish doing the tugging or a great big shark.

I carry floats in a multi-compartment plastic box that protects them from being chipped or broken. I carry the neoprene rubber beads for my slip floats in the same box, so everything is always together and organized. A few chunks of spare tubing for fixed floats go in the box too, since the stuff does dry out with age and occasionally needs to be replaced.

To load line on a spinning reel, lay the line spool on the floor flat on its side, so the line comes off the end of the spool. Run the line through the rod guides, tie it to the reel spool, and start cranking. To maintain sufficient tension while winding it on, hold the rod a foot or so up from the handle, and pinch the line between your thumb and forefinger as you crank it on with your other hand. If the line coming off the spool begins to tangle around the rod tip, then flip the spool over so the other side is facing up.

Fishing Line

Fishing lines are measured by their tensile breaking strength, expressed in pounds, such as eight-pound line, ten-pound line, twenty-pound line, and so on. An eight-pound line will break when eight pounds of strain is applied to it. A twenty-pound line will withstand twenty pounds of stress. It used to be called twenty-pound *test*—the word "test" evidently suggesting the line had been subject to some sort of certification. Although the term persists, there is no test, and you don't have to study.

It is important to understand fishing-line strength for what it is. It does not mean you cannot catch a nine-pound fish if you have only eight-pound line. If the reel's drag is set properly, it and the rod's spring action should prevent the fish from ever putting anywhere near eight

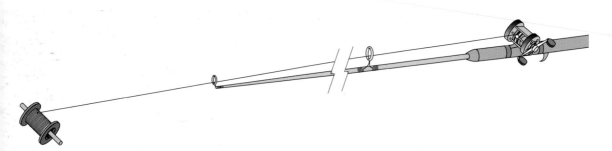

To load line onto a baitcasting reel or fly reel, you'll need the line to come off the spool as it rotates. Thread the line up the rod and tie it onto the reel spool, then have a friend shove a pencil through the line spool and hold it while you crank it on the reel. Maintain tension by pinching the line between thumb and forefinger as you crank it on with your other hand.

pounds of stress on your eight-pound line. This is why anglers have been able to catch enormous fish on even very light lines. For example, the International Game Fish Association, which maintains angling records worldwide, has documented numerous catches that appear impossible: a 632-pound (287 kg) blue marlin on sixteen-pound line; a 977-pound (443 kg) mako shark on thirty-pound line; and an enormous 1,068-pound (485 kg) great white shark on just twenty-pound line. Were it not for flexible rods and smooth drag systems in the reels, these catches could not occur.

Modern fishing lines are really quite remarkable. The most common type of line is monofilament—basically, a continuous length of thin, solid nylon extruded from a machine, almost like a length of spaghetti. Mono, as it's called for short, comes in a range of colors and in strengths ranging from one- to 130-pound. For freshwater fishing we're most concerned with lines of four, six, eight, ten, twelve, fourteen, seventeen, twenty, and twenty-five pounds.

Most of the mono sold today is clear, but it's also available in a range of tints, from dull green to brown, designed to better camouflage it from fish. Fluorocarbon line, which is a derivative of monofilament, virtually disappears in water and is unbeatable for fishing in very clear water. If fish can see the line, they're less likely to bite, so the subtle approach is a big plus. It is also possible to find so-called super-lines made from various braided materials, which offer unbelievable strength in a very small-diameter package. These lines do have some benefits, but they are comparatively difficult to cast and prone to tangle. At this point in time, monofilament remains the line of choice for most freshwater fishing applications.

Buying fishing line is like buying vegetables: freshness counts. Line loses strength as it ages, and exposure to sunlight will shorten its life faster than anything else. I never buy line from stores that have the stuff sitting anywhere near the front window. Fresh line will feel soft and supple in your fingers, where stale line is dry, crisp, and brittle. Old line will also coil like wild, making it almost impossible to cast.

When you put line on your reel, it is important to make sure you have enough. Typically, you want the line to come to about one-sixteenth of an inch (2–3 mm) from the edge of the spool. Too much line will result in incessant tangles, while too little will rob you of casting distance. You also want line to go on the same way it will come off when you cast, so it doesn't twist. With a spinning outfit you lay the line spool on the floor, flat on its side, so the line comes off the end of the spool. Run the line through the rod guides, tie it to the reel spool, and start cranking. To maintain sufficient tension while winding it on, hold the rod a foot or so up from the handle, and pinch the line between your thumb and forefinger as you crank the line on with your other hand. If the line coming off the spool begins to tangle around the rod tip, then flip the spool over so the other side is facing up. Baitcasting reels need the line to come off the spool as it rotates. Have a friend shove a pencil through the line spool and hold it while you crank it onto the reel. Again, maintain tension by pinching the line between thumb and forefinger as you crank it on with your other hand.

Properly loaded, the line should come to within about 1/16 of an inch (3 mm) from the edge of the reel spool. Too much line will lead to tangles when you cast; not enough will reduce casting distance.

Fishing line lasts a long time, but I like to replace mine as soon as it begins to show wear by becoming stiff and coily. Why risk losing the fish of a lifetime due to old, worn-out line? That would be penny-wise and pound-foolish.

Sunglasses

Hooks, lines, sinkers…and sunglasses? Yes. I consider a quality pair of polarized sunglasses to be an essential piece of tackle.

There are plenty of reasons for wearing quality sunglasses in the outdoors. First and foremost, they filter out those invisible, burning ultraviolet (UV) rays. Few people would head out for a day in the sun without first applying sunscreen, so it only makes sense that we should similarly protect our eyes. A good pair of sunglasses (along with a brimmed hat) fends off headaches and eye strain so we can enjoy our time outside without having to reach for the Tylenol at day's end. Sunglasses also provide a physical shield to keep objects from finding their way into your eyes. I look at the various dings and scratches in my sunglasses and wonder how many times they've kept sand, tree branches, and other debris from flying into my eyes. Perhaps the most talked-about benefit of wearing polarized lenses is that they cut glare so you can see through the water's surface and spot cover, weedlines, and, occasionally, even fish. I wouldn't even consider fishing in shallow water without them.

Unfortunately, a snazzy package that says Fisherman's Glasses is no guarantee the glasses will be worth a hoot on the water. In fact some of them can do more harm than good, even leading to permanent eye damage. This is one area where quality really counts. Glasses for fishing should filter out at least 97 percent of UV light. If they don't attain this minimum standard, don't buy them. Usually, glasses that offer this level of protection will be marked accordingly, although there are still no consumer standards for sunglasses in either Canada or the United States. If the product doesn't state that it absorbs UV, it probably doesn't.

Lenses come in two basic materials: glass and plastics. Glass gives the best optical quality and clarity, but it's also costly and heavy. High-grade plastic lenses have become increasingly popular because they're reasonably inexpensive and very lightweight. Good plastic lenses are almost as optically correct as glass and are more resistant to fogging. The only real downside to plastic lenses is that they're easier to scratch.

Whatever you choose, look for precision-ground lenses as opposed to cheap molded ones, which are often full of strain-causing distortions. You can get a good idea of what you're buying by looking through the lenses while slowly moving them around about a foot in front of you. Focus on a subject on the other side of the room and slowly move the sunglasses back and forth. You shouldn't see any movement of the subject itself—only the frames. If there's movement of the subject image, it indicates some distortion in the lens. And that's a warning: don't buy them.

Quality sunglasses come in a variety of colors to suit different light conditions. Green or gray lenses are easily the most popular among anglers because these tints do not appreciably affect color perception. I also like yellow or amber lenses for fishing in overcast weather or when I'm out at dawn or dusk. Yellow lenses make it appear lighter out than it really is and absorb a lot of UV glare. They're great in the rain, too.

A good pair of off-the-rack polarized fishing sunglasses starts at about $15, while top-of-the-line products may cost more than $200. As with anything else, you get what you pay for. You can't put a price tag on your sight, so investing in good fishing glasses makes a whole lot of sense any way you look at it.

CHAPTER 5

Fishing Lures

Artificial lures come in an astonishing range of colors, sizes, shapes, styles, and materials. It's awfully confusing. And why on earth wouldn't one just stick to using worms or minnows on a plain hook?

Artificial lures are popular for many reasons. Unlike bait, lures are reusable. One fish will make a mess out of a worm, but you can catch dozens, or even hundreds, of fish on the same artificial lure. Although a tackle box stuffed with lures represents a serious investment, over the long haul it's far less expensive than repeatedly buying bait. And a lot of the time, artificials are simply more effective.

There are other advantages to using fakes instead of real bait, chief among them the simple fact that a box of lures requires no care whatsoever. You don't have to keep them in a cooler, shade them from the sun, store them in the fridge, or change their water every hour or so. A small box of lures will fit in a big pocket, so you can be more mobile—a big consideration if you fish from shore or wade a stream. You don't have to worry about your bait flying off the hook should you make a rough cast. And it's doubtful you'll run out of bait. In some areas legislation prohibits people from using organic baits for a variety of reasons. Lures are the obvious answer.

So there are many reasons why anglers inevitably wind up buying artificial lures. But as you face a tackle shop crammed with all sorts of weird and wonderful creations, virtually every one of which will catch fish, how on earth do you decide what will work for you? Fishing lures can be divided into a variety of categories based upon their design, just as golf clubs fall into categories based on the type of job they're designed to do. I tend to carry groups of lures together in little plastic boxes with movable

The depth a crankbait can attain is determined by the size of its lip. These two Bomber Model A lures are identical in every respect except lip size. The top lure will reach a depth of about 10 feet (3.4 m). The lower lure, with its smaller lip, will only run about four feet deep.

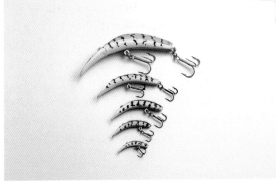

Many lures come in families, ranging in size from models suitable for sunfish and trout all the way to giant versions for trophy pike and muskie. The profile view of these Helin Flatfish lures shows why they're sometimes called banana baits.

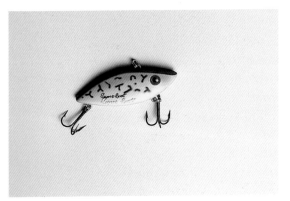

Rattlebaits like the Cordell Spot are ideal when you need to cover water and go looking for active fish.

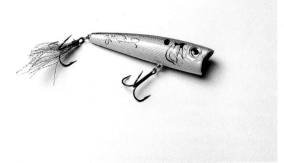

Poppers, like the Rebel Super Pop-R, are outstanding surface baits when fish hold tight to specific pieces of structure or cover. Fished in a slow stop-and-go, they're very effective lures.

Propeller lures such as this Heddon Dying Flutter emit a soft gurgling sound when retrieved. They can be worked fairly quickly for a topwater lure, making them good bets when fishing more expansive areas.

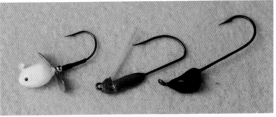

Most of the time, author Craig Ritchie goes with plain round ball jigs. But for special situations, he uses specialty heads like (from left to right): Lindy Little Joe's Lil' Hummer. The propeller adds a bit of flash and vibration, while slowing the jig's descent—a big plus in cold water; weedless jigs, for fishing in and around weeds or sunken wood; and stand-up jigs. With the eye located far forward, these types slip through grassy weeds without fouling.

dividers. When I pack for a day's fishing, I can then bring along only the types of lures I need, and can leave behind the ones that I won't. Why cart along salmon lures when I'm trying to catch bass? These compact plastic boxes go into a big bag or, if I'm stream-fishing and need the mobility, into a fishing vest with lots of big pockets.

Now let's take a closer look at the different varieties of artificial lures used for freshwater fishing in North America.

Crankbaits

By far the largest group of artificial lures, crankbaits get their name from the fact that you crank on your reel to work them through the water. Although they come in a wide range of sizes and shapes, all crankbaits have a body made from plastic, wood, or metal, a hook or hooks attached on little metal eyelets, and a lip or groove somewhere up front that imparts an erratic action as the lure is pulled through the water. Once more commonly known as plugs (the originals were hand-carved from wooden barrel plugs), the crankbait family includes short, squat lures commonly referred to as crankbaits and longer, more slender lures some anglers refer to as minnowbaits (because they're intended to mimic a baitfish). To keep it all simple, I refer to the entire family as crankbaits.

Jigs dressed with hair or feathers are the best choice for fishing in weeds or around submerged branches. Plastic bodies sometimes slip down the hook upon making contact with the weeds, ruining the presentation. Not so with hair.

Crankbaits will catch virtually any fish that swims. The biggest plus is that they work on a horizontal plane, so you can use them to cover quite a bit of water in a very short time (as opposed to lures like jigs, which work on a vertical plane and take a lot longer to cover the same amount of real estate). The old saying about 90 percent of the fish living in just 10 percent of the water is true, so the quicker you can find that magic 10 percent, the faster you'll start to catch something. Being able to cover water fast is one of the greatest benefits of fishing cranks.

You can also fish crankbaits at different speeds, from fast to slow to stop-and-go, and you can fish them at a variety of depths, from right on top to way down deep. Crankbaits closely mimic the number one natural food of most predatory fish: minnows, perch, and other smaller fish. You can also find crankbaits that resemble crayfish, frogs, you name it. Some of these look so lifelike, they're positively scary.

Looks aside, there are things to consider when selecting crankbaits. Let's examine these qualities in more detail.

Depth

Exactly how deep a crankbait will dive depends on several factors, but a quick clue is provided by looking at the lip. As a rule, crankbaits with great big lips dive deeper than those with little wee lips. Some manufacturers, including

Bomber, Rebel, Cotton Cordell, Mann's, and Rapala, produce what have become known as "series" crankbaits—the exact same lure offered in a number of different models, each with a different-sized lip. So you can buy the exact same lure in versions that run shallow, mid-depth, and deep.

But there's a lot more to a crankbait's depth than just lip size. Lip shape is a big factor as well. Hollowing out the front face of the diving lip gives a lure extra digging ability, sending it a foot or so deeper than one with a flat face.

Shallower-running lures such as the Bomber Square A and Cordell Big O feature squared-off lips, which are designed to allow you to bump the lure into rocks and logs without getting snagged. Crashing the lure into cover this way can be a deadly technique, especially when the fish develop lockjaw and ignore all else. The lip shape sends the lure bouncing away from the snags rather than digging in. Similar lures with rounded lips, like the Cordell Wally Diver and Rebel Shad-R, are better bets when you want to work the lure across a soft, sandy bottom and stir up some sediment. Rather than bounce off the sand, they plow right in and create a lot of commotion.

Modern crankbaits use plastic lips that are either molded with the lure as a single one-piece unit (as in the case of the Bomber Model A) or fitted and glued into place (as with the Rebel Minnow). Still others, like the Storm Hot-n-Tot, Lucky Strike Wooden Baits, and Creek Chub Pikie Minnow, use a metal lip, which you can bend to customize lure action. Lip construction and attachment doesn't matter, though—it's size and shape that determine how deep the lure will go.

Sometimes called minnowbaits in reference to their shape, slender crankbaits like the Smithwick Rogue are tops for species that prey heavily on smaller fish.

Speed

The lip style and size, along with the lure's body profile, will affect how fast or slow you can fish a given crankbait. Big lures with big lips can be worked fast, provided you're willing to crank like crazy and burn a lot of calories. Try working a big Hellbender or a giant Flatfish at top speed for more than a few minutes. You'll be begging for a break.

There's no question, fishing crankbaits fast can be a great way to catch fish. The trick from the angler's perspective is to select a lure you can work fast without wearing yourself out. That's when you want to go with lures that have slender lips. At 5½ inches (15 cm) long, a Rapala Super Shad Rap is a pretty big bait, but it's easy to fish quickly because of its neat lip design. For the sake of comparison, try reeling fast with a Bagley Monster Shad, which is about the same size and shape as the big Rapala; you'll be on the fast track to a hernia. The Bagley lure features a larger, broader lip, so working it fast takes far more effort on the angler's part.

When you need to go slow, lures with integral lips, formed directly into the lure body—such as the Flatfish, Lazy Ike, Tadpolly, and Kwikfish—are the way to go. The entire lure body acts as a lip, giving tremendous action at even the slowest speed. Sometimes jokingly called banana baits because of their curved shape, these lures are among the best fish-catchers of all time. They kick out a violent, throbbing action even at dead-slow speeds—a combination few fish can resist.

Action

When it comes to action, crankbaits invariably fall into one of two categories: wobblers and flashers.

Wobbling crankbaits—such as the Flatfish, Bomber Long A, Rebel Crawfish, Canadian Wiggler, Cordell Big O, Luhr Jensen Speed Trap, Heddon Tadpolly, and Rapala Fat Rap—display a violent left-right action when retrieved. Water moving over the lip forces the front of the bait from side to side, pointing the nose left, right, left, right, as it stammers along. This throbbing action causes a great deal of vibration and sound, making wobbling crankbaits ideal choices for use at night, in low-light periods, in off-colored water, when fishing in and around weeds, or in any other situation where fish may not be able to see the lure right away. The ability to generate tremendous amounts of vibration at very slow speeds makes these baits tremendously effective when fishing in cold water, when fish may be reluctant to chase a faster-moving lure. Models with integral rattles add even more noise and vibration.

Flasher-style crankbaits—such as the original Rapala, Cordell C.C. Shad, Storm Thin Fin, Smithwick Rogue, A.C. Shiner, and Rebel Minnow—tend to throw off more flash and glare, while emitting less sound and thump. These lures rely on visibility more than vibration, moving along in a straighter, more direct path, with the body rolling to show more belly, less belly, more belly, less belly. Flashers are often better bets in high-visibility situations, such as when fishing a very clear lake at midday, or when fishing for species like pike that are primarily sight-feeders. Flashers in toned-down, subtle colors can be just the trick for spooky fish that may shun the aggressive action of a wobbler. Sometimes the subtle approach works best. Because you can retrieve these lures very quickly, they're terrific when fishing in very warm water, where fish will eagerly and aggressively chase down prey.

When deciding to try one crankbait type or another, it really pays to think about the water temperature. Are you fishing in soup-warm water during a summer heat wave, or are you trying to catch late-season muskies in ice water? Remember: the warmer the water, the higher the fish's metabolism, and the more likely they are to chase an active, fast-moving lure. In colder water, when the fish have less zip, they're more likely to prefer something slower or more subtle.

Wood, metal, or plastic?

The manufacturers of wooden crankbaits like the Rapala or A.C. Shiner say that wood provides the most natural, lifelike action possible due to its natural buoyancy. The downside to wood is that its light weight makes it tough to cast these crankbaits into a wind, especially with baitcasting gear. Toothy critters like pike, muskie, chinook salmon, and even big lake trout can reduce wooden lures to mangled splinters in short order.

Most crankbaits today are made from plastic, which, being heavier, is generally easier to cast when the wind comes up. Manufacturers working with plastic, including Bomber, Rebel, Smithwick, Cotton Cordell, and Heddon, also find it easier to add rattles to plastic lures or make the lures suspend, while the molding process allows for a greater range of shapes and finishes. Plastics also tend to stand up to chewing a bit better than wood.

For the ultimate in durability you can buy metal crankbaits, like the Canadian Wiggler. Formed from tubular brass, these wobblers are just about indestructible. They produce a unique sound from the hooks bouncing against that hollow metal body, and cast like bullets even into hurricane-force winds. The downside to metal is that these lures sink like a rock, so they become an expensive choice in snaggy waters.

Shape

I've already mentioned that the crankbait family of fishing lures includes baits with body shapes ranging from something that resembles a pencil to something more like a golf ball. Still others look like bananas. I've always believed that the action of a given lure matters far more than its shape. But all else being equal, fish will sometimes exhibit a preference for one body style over another.

There are two basic guidelines when considering body shape. The first is to think in terms of the fish you want to catch. If you're targeting walleye, for example, and you know that in your particular lake walleye eat mainly minnows, you would be best off picking a crankbait with a long slender profile that mimics the profile of the most common prey item. This may seem obvious, but it's amazing how often the obvious gets overlooked. The second thing to keep in mind is that, as a general rule, omnivorous fish like bass will respond better to short, round, fat crankbaits than species like pike or walleye, which eat primarily fish and therefore tend to prefer longer, slimmer lures.

Buoyancy

Crankbait buoyancy refers to what the lure does at rest. Some float, some sink, others suspend in the water. Body shape and material can affect buoyancy. When you stop retrieving a short, rounded, hollow plastic crankbait, that lure will normally rocket to the surface. Stop retrieving a similarly sized, slender wooden crankbait and it too will float to the surface, but at a much more leisurely pace. A solid plastic lure may just sit there and neither float nor sink. One that's weighted will plummet to the bottom.

From day to day, fish may prefer one over the other, and you'll just have to experiment to find out. Active fish in warm weather will usually prefer something fast and lively, while on cooler days, or when dealing with less active fish, a slower approach will normally be the ticket.

Crankbaits that suspend at rest can be the ultimate for spooky fish, or fish that have seen a lot of lures. Years ago, professional bass tournament anglers used to doctor regular floating lures by adding weight to make them suspend. They then used these suspending lures to clean up on big fish when other anglers around them couldn't buy a hit. As a result, many manufacturers began to introduce suspending models of their more popular lures. If you don't own any suspending crankbaits, you are missing out. When conditions turn tough, they can work like magic.

Do crankbaits work? This rare photo shows a pike and a walleye each hooked on opposite ends of the same bait—a Bomber Long A.

Organization and selection

I carry crankbaits in my favorite boxes—those clear plastic ones with movable dividers—grouped by type. For example, one box contains nothing but lures that dive very deep. Within that box is a wide range of sizes, body shapes, floating models, suspending models, sinking models—you name it. But they all reach depths of fifteen feet (4.6 m) or more. I have a similar box for lures that work at between eight and fifteen feet (2.4 and 4.6 m), again in a wide range of styles and colors, and a third box of crankbaits that work at depths of eight feet (2.4 m) or less.

Having them organized this way makes it fairly easy to decide what to use. If I arrive at a spot that's twelve feet (3.7 m) deep, I pick the box of medium-runners and I've already narrowed my selection significantly. I'll then decide size and body shape based upon what kind of fish I want to catch, the water temperature, and how active I believe the fish will be. Finally, I make a decision on color based upon water clarity. Presto!

Rattlebaits

Some anglers call these lures lipless crankbaits, and that's a pretty fair description. Flat, roughly fish-shaped, and loaded with loud rattles, these lures vibrate rapidly from side to side on the retrieve, creating an enormous amount of noise and vibration. When you need to cover water, they're one of the best choices going.

Rattlebaits either sink or suspend at rest. The most popular way to fish them is to cast them over submerged weedbeds, or over shallow rocky flats, and retrieve them quickly and continuously. Rattlebaits are also tailor-made jigging lures; just let them sink to bottom, then retrieve in a steady hop-and-go.

Surface Lures

Some types of fish, in particular bass, pike, and muskie, frequently take food directly off the surface of the water. Fishing for these species with lures designed to work right on the surface is not only productive but incredible fun. It's called topwater fishing, and there isn't much in angling that's more exciting.

Surface lures are designed to imitate some poor critter that's helpless on the water surface: frogs, dying fish, snakes, even ducklings and baby muskrats. Most surface lures use a hard-formed body like a crankbait, with a concave surface at the front or little metal wings of some sort, or even miniature steel propellers so they make a gurgling noise when retrieved. Other surface lures are made of solid plastic or metal and need to be retrieved quickly to keep them on the surface.

Where crankbaits are wonderful lures to use when you want to cover vast areas in search of fish, topwaters are something you use when you're casting to precise, specific locations. They work so slowly that using them

A fine collection of Mepps spinners, suitable for everything from trout to bass to salmon to pike. This is a double-sided Plano box; the other side holds even more spinners in different sizes.

to cover water in an effort to locate fish is generally unpractical (buzzbaits being the sole exception—we'll look at them in a moment). Surface lures are typically summer lures, used when fish are actively feeding in relatively shallow water. You can reel them in continuously, or fish them in a seductively slow stop-and-go that just dares a fish to bite. It's usually best to experiment and let the fish show you what they want on a given day.

Surface lures are great when you're fishing in areas with lots of submerged weeds. Because they stay on the surface, they won't get caught in the vegetation. I had the opportunity to fish with Canadian professional curler Marilyn Bodough a few years ago on western Quebec's Lac Beauchêne, on a trip where topwater lures were the only way to go. Marilyn may be a champion curler, but at that time, fishing was entirely new to her. One magnificent, sunny June evening we fished a long, shallow bay for smallmouth bass. Clumps of thick pondweed were emerging everywhere, and I didn't want Marilyn to become discouraged by constantly getting her lure fouled in the vegetation. So I rigged her up with a Heddon Tiny Torpedo—one of my all-time favorite surface lures. The Torpedo would float above the plants without getting fouled, while attracting attention from hungry smallmouth bass.

We cut the motor as we entered the bay, and as the boat continued to drift forward, I instructed Marilyn to cast towards a long grassy point extending off the shoreline. Her cast was perfect, and the aptly named

Torpedo, which looks somewhat like a cigar butt with a little propeller on the back end, landed just inches from the end of the point. For a moment it sat there on the flat lake surface, the ripples it created upon landing drifting slowly away. I had told Marilyn to work the Torpedo back to the boat in a very slow stop-and-go. After about fifteen seconds she lifted her rod tip and crawled the lure forward about six inches (15 cm). The little propeller chugged away, leaving a wake of bubbles behind the lure. Again she let it sit till the ripples melted away, then slowly burped it forward.

Right on cue, a plump, lusty smallmouth of about three and a half pounds (1.6 kg) slammed into the lure. Marilyn screamed. The bass rocketed out of the water and danced across the surface, shaking its head wildly. The torpedo went one way, the bass the other, and Marilyn stood in the boat, wide-eyed and shaking.

"I think you have a bite," I offered.

After a few minutes Marilyn regained her composure, and she went on to catch several fine smallmouth with the Torpedo that night.

Clearly, fishing with surface lures is not for the faint of heart, or for those individuals with suspect internal plumbing. It's absolutely nerve-shattering, which is why so many people consider topwater fishing to be the most fun of all.

As I mentioned, topwater lures are best when you're fishing small, defined locations, such as along the edge of a weedbed, a significant drop-off, or a shallow bay. Topwaters are generally too slow to be of much use when you have to prospect for fish and cover a lot of ground. However, one type of surface lure—the buzzbait—is a notable exception.

Why fish attack buzzbaits is totally beyond me, for they look like nothing in nature. Basically a wire shaft with a small weight, a hook, and a bent chunk of metal that looks like the blade from a science-fiction windmill, you reel them across the surface at high speed, where that flat metal blade sputters, splashes, and does a fine impersonation of a miniature seaplane taking off. For reasons known only to our scaly friends, bass, pike, and muskie often find them simply irresistible.

There are two times when I use buzzbaits: when the fish are so active that they attack anything that moves, and when I am actively searching for fish and have to cover a vast area of shallow water. Those days when the fish will attack anything are few and far between, but when they come along, buzzbaits are the only way to go. I have a mangled Blue Fox buzzbait at home that survived a week of fishing at northern Manitoba's Munroe Lake a few years back. The lake's big northern pike were positively ravenous, and after the first day I didn't take the buzzbait off. It's been chewed on by so many fish, it barely functions and has no paint left on it. It also produced my best fish of the trip—a twenty-five-pound (11 kg) northern that plastered it in just a foot of water.

My box of surface lures includes a variety of styles and sizes, primarily poppers like the Rebel Pop-R and Arbogast Hula Popper, several propeller-style lures like the aforementioned Heddon Torpedo and the venerable Dying Flutter, as well as some cigar-shaped Zara Spooks. I don't get too hung up on color, as the only part of a topwater lure that the fish ever sees is the belly. Light-colored lures stand out against the surface of the water, so they're easier for me to see. I also like solid black lures, which stand out better against lighter-colored bottoms, such as sand.

A second box includes several buzzbaits in various sizes and colors. I like buzzbaits with twin blades, as I find the double blades allow me to work the lure more slowly while making all sorts of noise that attracts fish.

Spinners

If I were trapped on a desert island and could have only one lure, I'd give very serious consideration to making that one a spinner. They're incredibly versatile lures that will catch all types of fish. Spinners are strange-looking things in your hand. Picture a weighted wire shaft with a hook on one end and a floppy metal blade dangling off the side. But place the thing in the water and it's a different story. When you retrieve it, water pressure forces the blade to spin wildly around the wire shaft, beautifully mimicking a small fish. Spinners generate lots of flash thanks to their plated metal finish, as well as throbbing vibrations that attract fish from considerable distances.

Spinners can be found in sizes ranging from flyweight models of an inch or less in length to giant versions meant for muskies and trophy pike, a foot long and weighing several ounces. Unlike most other lures, spinners are generally not measured by their weight or length, but by the size of their blade. A tiny 00 blade is about the size of the nail on your pinky, while the big size 7 blades might be more than two inches (5 cm) long. Blade shape ranges from almost round (a Colorado blade) to long and slender (a Willowleaf). The shape of the blade determines how fast it will revolve and, subsequently, how deep the lure will go. Big round blades turn slowly and provide lift like an airplane wing, keeping the lure shallow at even slow speeds. Willowleaf blades, on the other hand, spin rapidly close to the lure body, and are a better choice when you want extra depth or are fishing in a very fast current. French-style blades fall somewhere between Colorado and Willowleaf styles, and represent a good compromise for all-round use.

Few lures can match the versatility of spinners. A few years ago a friend of mine named Jean Paul Daigle, who at the time was the marketing and advertising manager for Brecks International, the company that imports Mepps spinners into Canada, sent me several new spinners to try out, including one with a unique blue-and-silver pattern on the blade. Over the next two years I used that one spinner to catch steelhead in Ontario and British Columbia, smallmouth bass during a bass

Spinnerbaits and buzzbaits often benefit from the addition of a stinger hook. The author prefers the Lindy-style stingers, which feature a rubberized coating over the attachment eye to keep them from working loose. Treble hooks are even more effective as stingers when fishing in snag-free waters. Attach them as shown, with a small snap, secured in place with a piece cut from a rubber band.

tournament on northwestern Ontario's Lake of the Woods, walleye in northern Saskatchewan, big brook trout in central Quebec, and lake trout in Manitoba. I eventually lost the lure to a big pike on Lake Erie. I can't think of many other lures with that kind of versatility.

Because spinners sink like rocks, you fish them by casting and continuously retrieving. If you're fishing spots with a fair bit of current, it is possible to cast the spinner across the current and simply hold it on a tight line, allowing it to swing across the current, the water providing all the action. If you can get the lure to swing right over bottom, the blade tapping the stones, you will catch a lot of fish. It's a particularly effective technique for steelhead and coho salmon.

The only problem with spinners is that they have a tendency to twist the line. It's imperative to use a swivel—either attaching the lure to your line with a snap-swivel, or tying it on directly and splicing a small barrel or Crane swivel into your line six inches to a foot (15–30 cm) up from the lure. Failure to do this will leave your line twisted into unbelievable kinky coils that no amount of straightening will untangle.

I have two spinner boxes, one bristling with Mepps from the smallest size 00, for panfish and stream trout, to the largest size 5, for pike and muskie. A second spinner box contains huge lures like the Mepps Muskie Killer and the Magnum, designed specifically for the biggest fish in fresh water. Most have silver blades, but I also carry some with gold, copper, and black blades, which often work better on dull, overcast days.

Most spinners come with the hook left plain, or perhaps with the shank covered by a short length of bright plastic tubing. But it is possible to buy spinners with so-called "dressed" hooks, meaning the treble hook is wrapped with a mop of hair (usually squirrel tail or deer hair) that pulses through the water and adds a bit of bulk to the lure. I have become quite a fan of the dressed versions as I find the hair offers more bulk, increasing visibility, and it creates more resistance in the water, so I can work the lure more slowly at a given depth. I'm particularly fond of dressed versions of the bigger models, which I use for muskie and pike fishing, where there's enough hair to make the lure look a bit like a wet squirrel.

Spinners are tailor-made for tipping with bait, which can greatly increase their effectiveness in tough conditions. A snippet of worm added to the hooks gives the lure an appealing smell, making a good thing just that much better.

Spinnerbaits

A spinnerbait is one of the strangest-looking things you'll find in a tackle store. Imagine a V-shaped piece of wire that's tipped on its side, with a hook and a clump of silicone rubber fingers on the lower side, one or two spinner blades on the upper. They look like nothing Mother Nature ever devised, yet they catch fish with magical consistency.

Spinnerbaits are generally considered bass and pike lures, partly because of their ability to swim through even heavy weeds without getting snagged on the vegetation. I've caught a lot of muskie with them, a few walleye, and one misguided channel catfish, and have heard of people catching everything from panfish to steelhead to salmon on them. In other words, they're quite versatile.

Spinnerbaits are sized by weight, with lures weighing ¼ ounce, ⅜ ounce, ½ ounce, and ⅝ ounce the most useful for freshwater fishing. Much larger spinnerbaits in the ¾-ounce to 2-ounce range are used pretty well exclusively for big pike and muskie.

Spinnerbaits may come with a single blade, twin blades, or as many as four or five blades mounted along the wire shaft. The single-blade versions are my favorite for fishing in thick weed cover, because you can pause and let the lure sink down into any openings or along the edge of weedlines. The lure looks a little like a helicopter as it sinks with that blade whirling away above it, which is why some anglers refer to this technique as "helicoptering." When bass and pike are holding close to cover, it's a deadly approach.

Single-blade spinnerbaits are also the lure of choice when fishing at night, in muddy water, or in low light. That's when I want a *big* blade— the bigger the better—which kicks out as much vibration and plain old *whump* as possible. I watched a friend catch a number of beautiful largemouth bass once from a Georgia pond that was so muddy, the lure disappeared as soon as it hit the surface. There's no way a bass could see beyond a few inches in that soup, yet thanks to a slow retrieve and the incessant pounding vibration generated by the big blade, my companion managed to land a half-dozen gorgeous bass in just a few hours. Of course, he was using a specially modified spinnerbait with a blade almost as big as a cigarette pack.

The same technique worked for a friend of mine, James Mouryas, on a big, shallow lake two thousand miles away, on the swampy James Bay plateau in northern Ontario. While I shot photos for a magazine article on spinnerbait fishing, James coaxed a pair of monstrous northern pike— these fish each approached four feet (1.2 m) in length—from a grassy bay by helicoptering a bright green spinnerbait along the edge of a broken weedline. That he was rewarded with *two* once-in-a-lifetime fish, on consecutive casts, no less, should say something about the effectiveness of this technique.

When I face the opposite situation and want to use a spinnerbait to cover water in high-visibility situations, I'll select a tandem-bladed model, most often with twin Willowleaf-style blades. I can work one of these lures very rapidly, which allows me to fish quickly and cover a great deal of real estate in a very short time. Big tandem spinnerbaits are one of my favorite lures for muskie and smallmouth bass when the wind blows hard. Most anglers go out in windy conditions and immediately head for the sheltered lee shoreline, or tuck in behind islands where they can escape the breeze. Not me. I go to spots where the wind blows hard along the shore and cast big, heavy spinnerbaits with tandem blades very close to shore, quickly retrieving them just under the surface. Smallmouth bass and muskie feed aggressively in these situations, and the strikes will just about rip your arm off. Any color will do as long as it's white, with silver blades.

I often use a trailer hook on my spinnerbaits (and on buzzbaits too). A stinger is a second, supplemental hook that you add to the main hook in order to increase hooking efficiency. If I'm fishing in or around weeds, I'll use a single hook as a stinger. I buy the Lindy Little Joe ones with an oversized hook eye that's dipped in rubber for easy and secure attachment without any fuss. If I'm fishing open areas, I'll use a small treble hook instead. To keep it from falling off or coming free when I'm fighting a fish, I cut a short length of quarter-inch surgical tubing (available at any pharmacy) and slip it over the eye of the stinger hook. I then poke the point of the spinnerbait's main hook through the tubing and slide it on past the barb.

Spinnerbaits are normally made from a stiff spring wire. I've become a big fan of the newer, heavy-duty versions that use a wire shaft made from titanium alloy. Although they're much more expensive than the regular variety, the titanium shaft bends and flexes far more than the plain spring wire, retaining its shape even after considerable chewing. They just plain last longer. If you find you use spinnerbaits enough that you begin going through them, perhaps investing in a few titanium models isn't a bad idea.

Because of their weird shape and bulk, spinnerbaits can be tough to carry in a regular tackle box. I use a couple of compact, clear plastic spinnerbait boxes that each hold about two dozen lures. One or two of these fit into my big tackle bag when the need arises.

Spoons

Spoons look exactly like their name would suggest, and legend has it the first models were in fact formed by cutting the handles off silverware. When pulled through the water, spoons dart from side to side, generating a lot of flash and throbbing vibrations. They're popular and effective for a range of species. Because they're made from metal, spoons also sink like rocks. This characteristic makes them great choices when you need to fish deep or in a heavy current. Their weight also makes them popular with shore anglers, who may need all the casting distance they can get.

Spoons come in a huge range of sizes, generally measured by length, ranging from an inch or so to more than a foot. Most freshwater game fish respond to lures in the two- to six-inch (6–15 cm) range. Spoons also come in a range of shapes. As a general rule, narrow, thin ones work deeper than broad, squat ones.

On a press trip to northern Manitoba's Munroe Lake, organized by the Plano tackle company a few years ago, I spent an afternoon watching a fellow writer from Cleveland named Darcy Egan catch one trophy pike after another on a heavy yellow Dardevle spoon with red diamonds on it. I didn't have anything remotely like it with me, and was unable to get my own lures deep enough to keep up. Although I did manage to boat several big pike, Darcy was clearly outfishing me by about four to one with his heavy spoon.

Spoons are highly versatile lures. Those with pure silver or gold plating, such as the Williams, are most visible, even in dingy water.

Spoons come in a variety of thicknesses, which seriously affects not only the lure's weight but also its action. Generally speaking, thinner spoons tend to have more action than thick ones, all else being equal. Super-thin spoons, sometimes called flutter spoons, are made expressly for trolling behind the boat, and are so thin and lightweight, they're very difficult to cast.

Spoons are sold with a variety of finishes, including painted patterns, polished chrome or brass, and various types of reflective or phosphorescent tape. The brightest spoons I've ever seen, made by Williams, feature genuine gold and/or silver plating. Underwater you can see these lures coming from unbelievable distances, and I'm convinced that the pricey finish produces more fish, especially when angling in deep water where visibility may be limited.

Where most spoons have a treble hook attached to the rear end with a split ring, you'll also find some with a large single hook brazed to the belly, usually protected by a wire extending from the front. Called weedless spoons, these creations are designed to slip through submerged vegetation without getting snagged, and they're absolutely murder on weed-dwelling species like northern pike, muskie, and largemouth bass. Tip the hook with a soft plastic grub or a chunk of pork and you have a combination that's tough to beat.

For all-round freshwater fishing I'd suggest a variety of spoons ranging in length from about two to five inches (6–13 cm). That selection would be evenly split between models with narrow, moderate, and wide profiles. It's possible to find very inexpensive spoons in the bargain bin, but these cheapies never produce fish anywhere near as well as quality lures like the Dardevle, Len Thompson, or Williams. Besides being poorly made, the El Cheapo models inevitably come with flimsy fittings and low-quality hooks. By contrast, I can't even take a Williams out of the tackle box without stabbing myself with its needle-sharp hooks. Now that's money well spent!

Soft Plastics

In the past twenty years there have been more developments in the soft plastic lure category than in all others combined. These gooey creations make up one of my very favorite lure families.

The original soft plastic lures were designed to imitate real worms and frogs. These still exist, along with soft gooey crayfish, lizards, snakes, grubs, fish, cockroaches, and other things that don't look like anything in nature. And they all work. Freshwater fishing changed forever in the late 1960s and early 1970s with the introduction of the Mister Twister—a soft plastic grub about three inches (7.6 cm) in length, with a flat c-shaped tail that wriggled seductively when moved through the water. Rigged on a plain jig head, the Mister Twister began winning fishing tournaments and racking up record catches across North America. Within a very short time you could find them in all kinds of colors and sizes, from one to five inches (2.5–13 cm) in length. Dozens of companies scrambled to introduce their own version of the Mister Twister grub, in a dazzling array of colors, sizes, and configurations. Talk about an overnight success.

Today, the soft plastic grub remains a top seller and a top producer. I have caught pretty much every species of freshwater game fish on twister grubs, as well as several saltwater species. Fished on a jig head, or on a plain hook weighted down with a split shot or two a foot or so up the line, they're one of the most useful artificial lures of all time, and should be a staple in every angler's tackle box.

You can find grubs in a massive array of colors, but I tend to go with a variety of highly visible finishes like yellow, white, orange, and red, for fishing in off-color water, as well as a selection of more subtle lures in black, brown, dull green, smoke, and even clear plastic, for fishing in clear water. Most grubs sold today come with an artificial scent of some sort either added or impregnated into the plastic. I don't know if the scent helps or not, but it certainly doesn't hurt. The Berkley company's extensive Power Bait line are among the most successful scented grubs, along with the aforementioned Mister Twister and Riverside grubs.

A few grubs come with salt embedded into the plastic, and I'm convinced these are worth the extra cost. The theory is that fish taste the salt and believe it to be blood from their "victim." Perhaps so. I have found that fish will hold a salt grub in their mouth far longer than they will hold a non-salted lure, so perhaps there's some validity to the idea. I've even gone so far as to add salt to packages of grubs that come without it. The fact that so many tournament pros favor salt grubs over non-salted varieties tells me something about their effectiveness.

Tube lures, which resemble little octopuses or squid, came on the scene several years after twister grubs but now rival them in popularity. Tubes have a hollow body that tends to spiral as it sinks, giving the lure a unique action in the water. Rigged on a jig head, they've won countless major tournaments and put more than their share of trophy catches into the record books.

These soft plastic lures are most often fished on jig heads, but they can be rigged on a plain hook with a couple of split shot, or a slip sinker, a few feet up the line. Called split shot rigs, Carolina rigs, and drop shot rigs, these variations produce a lot of fish, especially in heavily fished lakes where doing something just a little bit different can have a huge impact on your success.

I buy tubes as I do grubs—a selection in bright colors as well as a selection in more subtle hues, again with a heavy preference towards lures with salt added. Like grubs, they come in convenient little plastic bags with zip closures, which keeps them neatly packed and easily accessible.

The latest craze in soft plastics involves what are commonly called slugs or soft plastic jerkbaits, named for the lure and technique that brought them to international prominence. When angler Herb Reed invented his original Slug-Go lure, he probably had no idea it would become one of the most copied designs in fishing history. A Slug-Go is a six-inch-long (15 cm) slab of soft plastic, shaped roughly like a flattened baseball bat. You rig it on a big single hook and twitch it through the water. By sharply popping it forward a few inches at a time with your rod tip, you can make the lure dart and swim very much like a dying baitfish. Sometimes fish hit lures tentatively, which suggests they're not entirely convinced the thing is actually edible. That's not the case with soft plastic jerkbaits. Fish typically engulf them in a lightning-fast, headlong rush. They're totally sold.

Soft plastic jerkbaits like the Slug-Go and its contemporaries, including the Power Slug and Big Gun, can be fished just as effectively on a plain hook with split shot or a sliding sinker, using them as substitutes for live bait. Called deadsticking, this technique of throw-it-out-and-wait has many followers, and has won its share of big-money bass tournaments in the United States and Canada.

Jigs

Because so many jigs rely on a soft plastic body of some sort as a dressing, there's a bit of overlap between this and the previous category. But jigs deserve special mention anyway, because they're far and away the single most versatile lure in the world. If I was stuck on that desert island with only one lure, I would choose a jig.

Jigs catch fish because they work on the bottom, where most of the fish are. A jig consists of two parts: a jig head, which is basically a hook with a lead weight molded onto it, and a dressing of some sort. The most popular dressings by far are soft plastic grubs and tubes, but other materials are also used. Before the advent of soft plastics, deer hair (called bucktail) and marabou (the soft underfeathers of a turkey) were the most

Few lures can match the versatility of a jig. Dressed with hair or feathers, or perhaps a soft plastic grub, they're tops for walleye, smallmouth bass and panfish.

popular jig dressings, wrapped onto the hook with stout thread. Both remain viable alternatives to soft plastics. Marabou in particular has a peculiar pulsing action on the water, which no other material can quite match. For super-spooky fish, it's still the final answer.

Jig heads are also used on their own, most often tipped with a live bait of some sort. Brightly painted jig heads offer the bait a flash of color for added attraction. Others, like the Lindy Lil' Hummer and the Northland Whistler, incorporate a little propeller on the hook shaft to make them fall more slowly in the water while adding a bit of flash and vibration.

Flipping jigs are a specialty item most often used for catching largemouth bass in heavy cover, but they also work magic on pike and muskie. Essentially a regular jig built on a super-heavy-duty hook and with a wire or fiber weed guard installed, they're very effective when lobbed into openings in weedbeds or in the shade of sunken trees.

Jig heads come in a wide range of shapes, all designed to do different things. Some have flattened bottoms that allow them to glide in the water, while others have flattened sides to help them sink faster in currents. Still others are bullet-shaped. Frankly, I find the plain round jig heads work for 99 percent of my needs. The sole exception comes when I'm fishing in weeds, where I use jig heads that have the hook eye set right at the front of the lead head. Positioned so, it's less likely to tangle in weeds.

Jig heads come in many colors as well. I like to have a selection of brightly colored heads for fishing in off-colored water, but I use black or plain, unpainted heads the majority of the time. It seems that bottom rocks chip the paint off most heads before too long, and in any case I want to draw attention to the dressing rather than the head. About the only time I use brightly painted jig heads is when I fish them bare, tipped only with bait.

For most freshwater fishing a selection of jigs from $\frac{1}{16}$ to perhaps $\frac{5}{8}$ ounce will suffice. I carry jig heads in a small Plano 3600 box, which fits anywhere and holds way more than I'll ever use on a single trip.

Scents

Scents aren't exactly lures per se, but as noted above, they're integrated into many commercially produced lures and sold as add-ons, in liquid and paste form. I began using commercial scents a few years ago and I've come to believe they do a lot more than just help cover my human odor. In certain situations scented lures will outfish unscented ones by a wide margin.

My first experiences with adding scent involved actual pieces of fish rather than the stuff sold in little plastic bottles. On a west coast salmon fishing trip several years ago, a friend and I drift-boated for early autumn chinooks, fishing huge Flatfish plugs that had chunks of herring carefully attached to their undersides. I asked the guide about the addition of the herring strip, as I felt the extra weight and bulk must interfere with the lure's action. He agreed, but said the additional scent more than made up for any loss of movement. And he proved it by fishing one rod the rest of the day with a bare lure. We hooked five salmon and missed three other hits—all on Flatfish with a herring strip attached. The bare lure went untouched.

On another trip, this time to a beautiful, remote lake in northern Ontario, the lodge owner suggested we jig for lake trout, using huge two-ounce (57 g) bucktail jigs tipped with a piece of sucker. Remembering our salmon trip the previous summer, my companion and I immediately began experimenting with scented and unscented jigs. The score for the week was more than forty lake trout on jigs tipped with a piece of sucker meat, only four on plain lures. That's when I became convinced of the value of scent.

Tipping lures with pieces of bait isn't new, but it isn't always easy or practical. It took about ten minutes to properly wrap the fish flesh to the belly of the Flatfish on the drift-boat trip. And the hardest part about tipping the jigs on our lake-trout trip was actually getting pieces of sucker to use. Keeping baits fresh on a hot day is a job all to itself, and that's part of the reason that commercial scents have become so popular in recent years. Bottled scents give you all the benefits of using real meat to tip your lures, but without the fuss and without otherwise affecting your lure's action or hooking ability.

More than a decade ago biologists discovered that human skin naturally secretes a matter called L-Serine. They also discovered that L-Serine repels fish. The precise amount of L-Serine secreted varies from one person to the next, which may explain why one person in a boat can catch all kinds of fish while his two buddies can't get a bite, despite using the same lures in the same spots. The lucky angler may in fact be secreting less L-Serine than his companions. Scents help improve one's catch rate by blocking out that human odor.

Other scent products try to improve your success by replacing your human odor with one that fish will find more inviting. It's one thing for your lure to *look* like a bait fish; if it also *smells* like one, your chances of eliciting a strike more than double. Some scent products even help your lures *taste* like real food items. This is a big plus, especially with soft plastic lures that are generally fished with a single hook. The longer a fish holds your lure in its mouth, the better your odds of getting a solid hook set. Fish can spit out things that don't taste right far faster than most anglers can react, so you want the fish to hold your lure as long as possible.

Scents normally come in either a squeeze bottle for direct application to lures, or a bottle with a pump mechanism for spraying. Judging by the shelves in major tackle stores, the pumps apparently outsell the plain bottles. I prefer to buy scent products in bulk bottles and simply pour an appropriate amount into an old margarine container, allowing me to dip my lure in every few casts and avoid getting the stinky stuff all over my fingers. There's nothing worse than stopping for a bite to eat on the way home from a fishing trip and having fingers that stink of crayfish or worms, no matter how thoroughly you wash them.

One trick used by many tournament anglers is to "adjust" their lures so that they hold scent for a longer period of time. Stuffing little pieces of foam rubber into tube jigs, then pouring the scent inside, is one technique that helps them hold their flavor longer. Using "fuzzy" jig heads covered with velour to help hold scent is another option. When fishing with hard baits like crankbaits or spoons, some tournament pros replace the factory treble hooks with new dressed versions, sporting skirts of feathers or hair. The dressing on the hooks holds scent longer.

Regardless of whether they squeeze it on, spray it on, or dunk their lures in it, many anglers feel that scents and attractants make a big difference in the number of fish they catch. By masking unpleasant smells— human odor, sunscreen, bug repellent, gas, tobacco, and oil—and replacing them with scents that entice fish to bite, these products give the angler a big edge. And who wouldn't like to catch a few extra fish?

CHAPTER 6

Rods and Reels

Modern fishing rods and reels are truly magnificent examples of contemporary engineering, combining age-old principles with materials derived from the aerospace industry. Even an outfit of moderate price and quality boasts enough high-tech engineering to make a top-of-the-line rig from the 1970s feel like a club by comparison. Rods and reels nowadays are incredibly lightweight, strong, and reliable.

The trick to buying a rod and reel is to buy tackle that is balanced, meaning the rod and reel are designed to work together. Balanced tackle is a joy to use; it casts effortlessly and feels good in the hands. Unbalanced tackle is quite the opposite: you'll have no end of problems trying to cast any kind of distance, and the outfit will inevitably feel awkward to use. Taking a small reel designed for trout fishing and mounting it on a heavy saltwater rod designed for tuna and sailfish just doesn't work. Happily, tackle companies have gone the extra mile to make the job of selecting balanced gear easier than ever. Most rods and reels come with the range of lure weights and fishing-line strength they are designed to handle printed right on them. If you decide on a rod that's designed to handle lines from ten- to twenty-pound test, then it's easy to find a reel designed for the same line range. Just read the label.

I like to think of fishing rods and reels the way golfers think of their clubs. They all do different jobs. Yes, you can putt with a driver or a pitching wedge, but

Spinning gear is the best choice when you need to cast lightweight lures, when using lightweight lines, or any time you need extra casting distance, such as when fishing from shore.

you probably won't have much success. This is why you will sometimes see professional tournament anglers with twenty or thirty rods in their boat. Each is set up for one specific job.

When you look at buying a rod and reel, it's important to be honest about how you will use it, and a lot of that is determined by where you fish. Forget about cosmetics, gimmicks, and flashy advertisements in fishing magazines. Ask yourself some basic questions and be honest in your answers. How large are the fish you actually catch (as opposed to the ones you dream about catching)? And how do you fish? Do you cast from shore? Or do you troll with a boat? Do you fish small streams that flow through thick brush, or do you fish on wide open lakes? Do you fish in calm, quiet areas, or do you often face strong winds that can make casting difficult? And what kinds of fish are you most likely to encounter?

The answers to these questions will determine what sort of rod and reel you should consider buying. To go back to our golf club analogy, if you really spend most of your time putting, it doesn't make much sense to buy a driver, does it? Similarly, a rod and reel designed to cast long distances into heavy winds won't give you any advantage whatsoever if you spend most of your time fishing for trout in tiny forest streams. So why pay for those features you won't make use of?

Happily, rods and reels aren't quite as specialized as golf clubs, and the manufacturers have done a tremendous job creating all-round outfits that can perform a variety of duties equally well. For a new angler, they're absolutely the best choice. Over time you may find you develop special fondness for one style of fishing or another, and when that happens, you can buy specialized rods and reels designed expressly for that type of fishing. For now, though, let's look at the different types of rods and reels one can expect to see in a typical tackle store.

Spinning Outfits

A fishing rod doesn't look like much when you hold it in your hand, but appearances are deceptive: modern rods incorporate tremendous levels of engineering and manufacturing expertise. In rods, it's what you *don't* see that makes all the difference. Subtle factors like the material used in its construction, the placement of guides, construction technique, components, and taper—internal and external—all play a hand in how a given rod performs. Forget about the shiny finish or the fancy thread wrap above the handle; they may look nice, but these things mean nothing in actual use.

One of the best ways to buy a fishing rod is with your eyes closed. As a general rule, your hands will tell you a lot more than your eyes will. How a rod feels when you hold it is much more important than its color or whether it's got a shiny or a matte finish.

Spinning rods and reels, sometimes called open-face outfits, are a

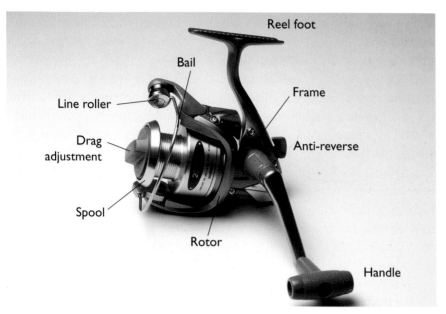

Labels on image: Reel foot · Bail · Frame · Line roller · Drag adjustment · Anti-reverse · Spool · Rotor · Handle

Principle parts of a spinning reel include the reel foot, anti-reverse, handle, rotor, bail, line roller, spool and drag adjustment.

European invention and first became popular in North America after the Second World War. Many of the first outfits were brought home by returning soldiers. Since that time spinning gear has grown to become by far the most popular type of rod and reel worldwide.

The two main benefits of a spinning outfit are ease of use and ability to cast even very lightweight lures great distances. A spinning reel stores line on a spool that is mounted parallel to the rod. When you cast, line peels off the end of the spool, as opposed to having the spool itself revolve to feed out line. This arrangement allows the line to flow off the spool with minimal friction, enabling even relatively inexperienced anglers to cast surprising distances, and without fear of the line tangling.

Because a spinning reel hangs under the rod rather than sitting on top of it, spinning outfits balance very nicely in the hand. You grip a spinning outfit around the reel foot, so the stem sticks out between your second and third fingers. To cast, you simply hook the line on your index finger, open the reel bail, flex the rod forward sharply, and, when the rod tip arrives at about a ten o'clock position, point your finger at the target, releasing the line. *Voilà!*

Spinning reels come in a range of sizes capable of handling everything from tiny panfish to sharks and giant marlin. For most freshwater fishing, a reel that can hold something like 175 yards (160 m) of six-pound line or 120 yards (110 m) of eight-pound will work just fine. All reels state their line capacity right on the box (and often on the reel itself), so it's easy to find one that's the right size. A reel that holds more line than that will also work just fine, but it will inevitably be larger, heavier, and probably more expensive. Why pay for features that you probably won't use? A reel with less line capacity may prove to be too limited. You won't be able to fish for species like salmon, pike, larger trout, or striped bass, which all tend to peel out line during the fight. A particularly large fish might just take off with all your line, leaving you holding an empty reel.

Over the past decade or so, reel manufacturers have begun marketing ambidextrous reels, where the crank handle can be mounted on either side to accommodate left- or right-handed anglers. Usually this is accomplished by removing a small retaining screw opposite the handle; the handle then pulls straight out, is reinserted through the opposite side of the reel, and the retaining screw is replaced.

Once you've found a couple of reels that appear to have the right line capacity, your decision on which one to buy essentially comes down to cost. More expensive reels will be better sealed against sand and dirt, and have better-quality gears and components throughout. They will also have better drags, and that's a key feature.

Drag is the common name for a slipping clutch mechanism built into fishing reels. When you hook a fish and it tries to swim away, it will put force on the line and something will have to give; either the line breaks or the hook pulls out. The drag prevents either of these things from happening by yielding line under pressure. A properly adjusted drag will surrender line to the fish before it ever reaches the breaking point. As the fish streaks away, you can usually hear the drag working, as most incorporate an audible clicker device. Some reels have the drag control mounted at the front, right on the spool, while others have it located at the back. The location is irrelevant. What matters is that it functions smoothly. Improved functioning of this drag mechanism, through higher-quality materials and the use of more and larger washers, is one element that contributes to a reel's cost.

You will also find that more expensive reels incorporate one or more ball bearings in their construction. Ball bearings allow the reel to turn more smoothly than is possible with traditional brass bushings. Generally, the more ball bearings, the more smoothly the reel turns. Some top-grade reels have as many as eight ball bearings; three to four is normally the mark of an excellent reel.

A good-quality spinning reel will provide many, many years of service. Although you can buy a decent reel for as little as $40 Canadian (about $25 U.S.), I usually recommend that beginning anglers spend a bit more and look at reels in the $60 to $80 range ($40 to $60 U.S.). While you may spend a little more up front, the result is a much better quality reel that will probably last twice as long as the cheaper one, while being more enjoyable to use the whole time.

The latest trend in spinning reels has been a return to the use of metal casings. For the past twenty years reels with graphite frames have been the rage, due largely to graphite's high strength and light weight. Now, metal is making a big comeback. The advantage of metal reels is that they have virtually no give. You can put all the stress in the world on them and they will not flex. Flex in the frame can allow the gears to move ever so slightly out of alignment, resulting in reduced performance and premature wear. For anglers who fish a lot, metal reels are the way to go. Although slightly heavier than graphite reels, modern metal reels are still significantly lighter in weight than their ancestors, thanks to modern high-strength alloys and improved manufacturing techniques.

Spinning reels should be used with spinning rods, which are recognizable by their rather large guides and straight handles devoid of a finger hook or trigger. Rods range in length from four to twelve feet (1.2–3.7 m), with six- to seven-foot (1.8–2.1 m) models the most popular. Rods shorter than six feet (1.8 m) are just plain difficult to cast, and are best reserved for fishing in tight quarters—such as the confines of a tiny trout stream flowing through a dense forest—where any additional length would prove awkward to handle. Longer rods are simply a pain in the neck to transport.

The safest way to carry several rods together is to bundle them with commercially-made rod wraps or self-adhesive tensor bandage, sold in drug stores. This keeps the rods together and prevents them from banging around, possibly nicking a rod blank or chipping an eye.

One-piece rods provide the greatest strength and sensitivity. However, once we exceed a length of about seven feet (2.1 m), they become extremely awkward to transport. Two-piece rods, which push together, are the answer here, and are popular in shorter lengths too, especially among anglers who travel a lot or who have smaller vehicles.

Pack rods, which comprise several sections, offer superb portability, but it comes at the expense of sensitivity and strength. If you really need a rod that fits inside a suitcase, they are the answer; but they're never as pleasant to use as a standard one- or two-piece rod. Telescopic rods, which have several pieces that fold together inside one another, are about the worst design, and are seldom offered by quality rod makers. (Do not confuse telescopic rods with specialty flipping sticks, used for bass fishing in heavy cover, which compress at the handle for easier transport.)

Most spinning rods sold today are made from a mixture of graphite and fiberglass. Graphite is an extremely lightweight, strong, and sensitive material, but it's also brittle as dry spaghetti, so its use in fishing rods almost always involves binding it with other materials. Rods with a high graphite content provide unmatched sensitivity but carry an unmatched price tag to go with it. Pure fiberglass rods are inexpensive and tough as nails, but about as sensitive as a wet newspaper. Glass-graphite composite rods provide a wonderful balance of sensitivity and affordability. A good spinning rod will cost about $50 to $70 Canadian, or about $35 to $50 U.S.

Fishing rods are measured by *action*, which means the rod's relative stiffness. A fast-action rod bends primarily in its thin tip section, while a

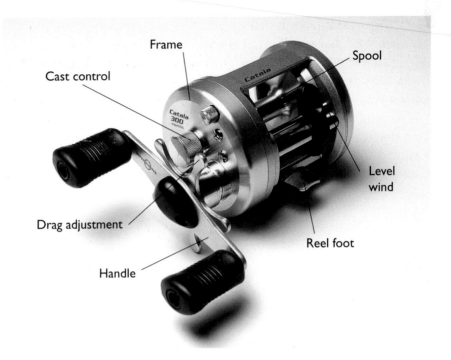

Principle parts of a baitcasting reel include the reel foot, handle, cast control, spool and level wind. Not visible in this photo is a thumb bar at the back of the reel, which disengages the gears for casting.

Frame

Cast control

Spool

Level wind

Drag adjustment

Reel foot

Handle

slow-action rod bends evenly right down to the handle. The action affects not only how the rod will cast but its ability to fight fish. As a general rule, fast-action rods are easier to cast, while slow-action rods are more efficient at fighting fish. The medium-action rod represents a logical compromise and is the best choice for one's first fishing rod.

Rods that taper quickly, meaning the diameter quickly lessens from being quite large at the handle to very small at the tip, behave differently than rods that maintain a more consistent diameter throughout their length. Whether the rod has more or less power is really determined by how abruptly that taper is structured. Rods with a very abrupt, or fast, taper tend to have tremendous power, while those with a less aggressive taper are better suited to handling light lines due to their increased flexibility. Again, a compromise—a moderate taper—is best for an all-round rod.

The rod's action also affects the range of lures it will be able to cast. Any fishing rod will be limited in the lure weights it will be able to cast. Some are designed specifically to cast very light lures, while others are meant for handling heavier baits. As most freshwater fishing lures weigh somewhere between ⅛ ounce and ⅝ ounce (3.5 g and 18 g), it makes sense that a starter outfit should be able to handle lures in that weight range.

Some rod manufacturers try to make it as simple as possible to select a rod and reel that are appropriate to your needs, and some even go so far as to list the optimum fishing-line strength and lure weight that their different rods will work with, printing this information right on the rod itself. This makes it easy to find a rod that will handle the range of lures you wish to use and work well with the six- to eight-pound line you'll be using on your mid-sized spinning reel.

When you spend more money to buy a better-quality fishing rod, you get better-grade components and a higher graphite content. The graphite itself will often be of a higher grade as well, greatly increasing sensitivity and strength while substantially reducing weight. For example, one of my rods is a top-of-the-line Shimano V-series, six and a half feet (2 m) long, able to handle fifteen-pound line and capable of subduing the biggest pike, bass, and walleye. Yet this powerful rod weighs far less than the average six-foot (1.8 m) spinning rod. Unfortunately, it also costs $150 more. For now, though, a basic mid-priced rod and reel, both of which are designed to handle six- to eight-pound line and lures from ⅛ to ½ ounce (3.5–14 g), will do just fine. This is a perfect starter outfit and can handle 90 percent of the freshwater fishing situations you are likely to encounter in North America.

Baitcasting Outfits

In many parts of North America the baitcasting outfit is king. The term *baitcasting* is actually somewhat misleading, because these rods and reels are far better adapted to cast artificial lures than bait. However, the term persists to this day.

Baitcasting rigs are a purely North American invention. The reel sits atop the rod, with the spool mounted perpendicular to the rod blank. To cast, you press a button or click a lever on the reel to disengage the line spool from the gears, and hold it stationary with your thumb. You raise the rod overhead and then sharply flex it forward. When it's more or less pointing at the target, you simply lift your thumb. The weight of the lure will cause the reel spool to revolve very quickly, playing out line that travels up the rod and follows the lure to its target.

The one big problem with baitcasting reels is that, once your lure lands in the water, the spool keeps right on turning, spitting out line that begins to bunch up in the rod guides. The inevitable result is a huge tangled mess, called a backlash or bird's nest. You then spend the next several minutes with a knife cutting it all apart. The trick to avoiding the backlash lies in educating your thumb. As the lure nears the target, you begin gently to touch your thumb to the spool, using it as a brake to keep the line from over-running and tangling once the lure hits the water. Most modern baitcasting reels have different types of magnetic and mechanical brakes designed to prevent backlashes. They all work to one degree or another, but the trade-off is reduced casting distance. The bottom line is, there's no substitute for an educated thumb. And that, unfortunately, comes only with practice.

Anyway, why go through all this hassle when you can escape these problems entirely with a spinning outfit? Well, the simple fact is, for fishing with heavy line in the twelve- to thirty-pound class, or for fishing in heavy cover where precise casts are necessary, the baitcasting outfit is unbeatable. Once you learn to feather the spool with your thumb, you'll find that baitcasting outfits are not only easy to cast but also far more accurate than any spinning outfit. When you're fishing in heavy weeds for largemouth bass or pike, for example, and need to drop your offering into a small opening the size of a soup bowl, you can do it with a baitcasting rig. They're also wonderful for trolling and for handling heavy line, which tends to become wiry in use, especially when it's cold.

Top-of-the-line baitcasting reels are likely to feature one-piece frames, which offer tremendous strength and light weight. Stealing a design concept from the reels used by big-game saltwater anglers, these one-piece designs are as close to bulletproof as a fishing reel can get. Although they do cost more than reels assembled from multi-piece frames, most anglers agree they're worth the extra cost. Properly cared for, they will last a lifetime.

I would not advise buying a baitcasting outfit as a first rod and reel unless you live in a place where the only fishing available involves pulling large fish from thick, heavy cover. But because they are unmatched at handling heavy lines and big fish, at some point most anglers will want to have a baitcasting rig, regardless of where they live. They're just too efficient at some things, and too enjoyable to use.

Because the cast relies on a rotating spool, baitcasting reels tend to have more parts than spinning reels, making them more complex and, of course, more expensive. Most incorporate at least one ball bearing, and more often three to five, while higher-end reels (read "more expensive") utilize some sort of super-free arrangement to allow for easier spool rotation. A typical baitcasting reel will hold somewhere around 170 yards (156 m) of ten-pound line or 125 yards (114 m) of fourteen-pound. Larger-capacity reels are useful for trolling, or for catching species like steelhead or salmon, which tend to strip a lot of line off the reel when fighting.

The drag on a baitcasting reel is normally adjusted by a star-shaped wheel found mounted on the same stem as the handle; turning it in one direction or the other either increases or decreases drag. Some reels have an audible clicker device so you can hear when the drag surrenders line.

Because of the intricate gearing, baitcasting reels do not lend themselves to being ambidextrous, as spinning reels do. However, many manufacturers offer their most popular reels in both left- and right-hand versions. You can buy baitcasting reels for as little as $40 Canadian ($25 U.S.), but these seldom perform well. Expect to spend somewhere between $125 and $150 Canadian, or in the $80 U.S. range, for a fairly good one.

Baitcasting reels sit atop the rod, so baitcasting rods normally have a small hook or trigger mounted on the bottom side of the handle, allowing a pistol-type grip with the forefinger. Because the line comes off the reel in a relatively straight line, the guides on a baitcasting rod are typically much smaller in diameter than those on a spinning rod, which helps reduce weight. Like spinning rods, baitcasting rods come in a range of actions and are designed to handle lures and lines within a specific range. While it is possible to find light-action baitcasting rods that can handle lines as light as six-pound, most are intended for lines from ten- to twenty-pound, which better suit the capabilities of baitcasting reels. Baitcasting rods range in length from five to ten feet (1.5–3 m), with six and a half feet (2 m) the most popular size. Most are of a graphite-fiber-glass composite construction. A good baitcasting rod costs about the same as a spinning rod of comparable quality.

Spincasting Outfits

Spincasting reels came into popularity in the 1950s, and were designed to combine the simple operation of spinning gear with the strength and ruggedness of baitcasting gear. A spincasting reel mounts on a regular baitcasting rod. A spincast reel works very much like a spinning reel, except that it sits atop the rod and the spool is encased in a conical metal or plastic shroud (which gave rise to the term closed-face reel, differentiating it from a proper spinning reel). Casting is accomplished by pushing a button on the back of the reel. When the rod is powered forward, you release the button and the line peels off the reel in the same way it would on a spinning reel. Because the spool arrangement is borrowed from spinning reel designs, the backlash problem doesn't exist. Overall, the reel looks somewhat like an egg with a button on one end, and the first ones were laughingly referred to as beer cans.

Although a great idea, spincasting reels have serious limitations inherent in their design. Taking the line off the end of the fixed spool and immediately forcing it through a small hole on the front of the reel limits casting distance and accuracy. Furthermore, the orientation and location of the spool make it difficult to accommodate anything more than a rudimentary drag system. Line capacity is also rather limited, and should a tangle develop, you have to take the front shroud off the reel to sort it out. The shrouded arrangement also makes it very difficult to incorporate basic mechanisms like oscillating line winding—a standard feature on almost all spinning and baitcasting reels, where the line wraps on the spool at an angle, to keep it from digging in under itself when subjected to stress.

With the exception of a handful of models, most spincasting reels sold today are cheaply made, simple affairs intended for very casual anglers or kids. I dislike them, and strongly suggest that anyone getting started in fishing buy a regular spinning outfit instead. The standard spinning reel is every bit as easy to use, yet typically features a much better drag and far greater line capacity. It's also exceedingly more versatile.

Baitcasting outfits are best for heavy-duty fishing. The author prefers a medium-heavy baitcasting outfit when tangling with big fish, such as this 42-inch (108 cm) Saskatchewan pike held by Wollaston Lake guide Pete Orhirko.

Fly Outfits

Rods and reels used for fly fishing differ dramatically from conventional tackle. With a spinning or baitcasting outfit, you cast the weight of the lure or sinker. But because the flies used in fly fishing weigh very little, you cast the weight of the line instead. This greatly affects the way the rods and reels are built.

I will cover fly tackle and casting techniques in detail in the next chapter. In a nutshell, the fly reel is generally not involved in casting at all, but functions only as a place to store spare line. Accordingly, most are extremely simple when compared with spinning or baitcasting reels, consisting of little more than a large, rotating spool on a lightweight frame. The fly reel hangs under the rod and is normally mounted on the end of the rod, behind the handle, giving a fly outfit remarkable balance. Better-quality fly reels may incorporate features such as machined frames, ultra-smooth disc drags, and large-arbor spools, which allow more rapid line retrieval. Some fly reels are geared, for even faster line recovery.

Fly rods incorporate complex tapers to allow them to cast heavy lines a considerable distance, even in windy conditions, yet still have power left over to fight big fish while remaining lightweight and comfortable to use. They range widely in weight, length, and power, with the most popular ones for North American freshwater fishing falling somewhere between eight and nine feet (2.4 and 2.7 m) in length, with sufficient power to cast big, bushy flies into a stiff wind and fight fish as large as pike or salmon.

A high-end fly fishing outfit can cost big money—into the thousands of dollars. However, a very good quality rod and reel combination that's capable of handling most freshwater fishing situations can be had for about $150 Canadian ($100 U.S.). That's a pretty fair deal.

CHAPTER 7

Fly Fishing

F ly fishing may well be the original means of catching fish for fun. Historical accounts of fly fishing go back thousands of years before Christ. In northern Europe and the United Kingdom, nobles tempted trout and salmon on crude hooks wrapped with bits of wool, feathers, and hair more than four thousand years ago. To say fly fishing has a rich and colorful history would be the understatement of the year.

Fly fishing remains popular for two simple reasons: most fish eat insects at some point in their life, making them susceptible to being caught on flies, and more importantly, it's just plain fun. Tens of

Fly fishing is the oldest form of recreational fishing, dating back more than 4,000 years. Yet it's still an effective approach today, particularly when fishing in moving waters such as creeks and rivers – including those flowing through urban areas.

thousands of people became inspired to try fly fishing after watching Brad Pitt in *A River Runs through It*. When you catch a fish on a fly rod, it's just you and the fish, with no weights, bobbers, geared reels, or anything else to come between you and it. Landing a big fish on fly gear is a feat to be proud of. Although the long springy rods do absorb a lot of energy in the fight, and provide terrific leverage for steering fish around snags and obstacles, it's still a challenge to bring a big fish to net.

Where fly fishing was once exclusively a technique for trout and salmon, particularly in streams, modern fly anglers have flattened all boundaries, and in the last sixty years have begun taking on all kinds of fish, including the largest sharks, sailfish, tuna, and marlin. In fresh water, fly fishing is a highly enjoyable way to catch just about all species that can be found in relatively shallow water, including largemouth bass, smallmouth bass, panfish, pike, and muskie. Although it is possible to take deep-dwelling species like lake trout and walleye with fly gear, specialist techniques and tackle are needed. Frankly, it's easier to catch those fish with a spinning rod, so we're not going to get into that here. All tackle has limitations of some sort, and that's certainly true of fly tackle. For fishing any deeper than about ten feet (3 m), or when you have to repeatedly make very long casts, stick with spinning gear; you'll enjoy more success and experience far less frustration. But for pure fun when fishing in fairly shallow water, fly fishing for bass, pike, muskie, perch, sunfish, trout, and salmon is extremely enjoyable.

The Basic Outfit

Like any other form of angling, you can make fly fishing as simple or as complicated as you wish. I prefer to keep things simple. Life is complicated enough as it is, and I fish to escape all that fuss.

The basic fly fishing outfit consists of rod, reel, line, leader, tippet, and backing, along with some flies. Let's look at it one piece at a time.

Fly rods are typically longer than rods used in other forms of fishing, normally between eight and nine feet (2.4 and 2.7 m) in total length, with a short handle and a terminal reel seat. The reel hangs beneath the rod, where it balances best. Almost all rods today are made of some mixture of graphite and either fiberglass or synthetic resins. You can buy a very good fly rod for about $40, though it's possible to spend $1,000 or more on a really high-end rod (if you just happen to have money to burn). Much of that higher price reflects prestige and cosmetics rather than actual improvements in performance.

The guides on a fly rod are most often formed from a loop of stainless steel wire, and are known as snake guides. This design is not only lightweight but also highly flexible—a plus in maintaining a smooth rod action. Most often the tip guide and base, or stripper guide, are of the traditional frame-and-ring style, usually with an insert made of some type of hardened alloy or silicone oxide. Better-quality fly rods use tiny single-foot silicone carbide guides throughout. These guides are far more expensive than the traditional steel snake guides, but allow easier casting and greater distance. Whether the added expense is worth incurring or not is, of course, a personal decision. It depends how much you use the rod. I would suggest buying a basic rod to begin with, moving up to a higher-end model if you find you use it enough to warrant the extra cost.

Fly reels come in a bewildering assortment of styles and configurations, but for the kind of freshwater fishing we're concerned with here, a basic single-action reel will do the job just fine. The term "single-action" implies the reel has no gears, so turning the handle once will result in the line spool turning once—in other words, it's direct drive. These are the lightest and simplest reels. Geared reels, which allow for faster line retrieval, are useful when fishing for fast-moving saltwater game fish, but they are far heavier and much more expensive, and not necessary for most freshwater fishing situations.

Similarly, while reels with sophisticated disc drag systems are wonderful when fishing for strong fighters that peel out lots of line, the truth is that the average bass or trout rarely goes more than twenty or thirty feet (6 or 9 m). Within the confines of a small to medium-sized river, even salmon aren't terribly difficult to handle with a single-action reel. My view is that for the majority of freshwater fishing applications, disc drag reels aren't worth the extra cost.

One feature that *is* worth looking for, however, is a palming ring: a raised lip on the end of the line spool that overlaps the reel frame and gives you a surface where you can press your palm to apply more pressure on a running fish. Should you hook something much larger than you expected, the palming ring allows you to judiciously apply as much pressure as you need. Reels with palming rings generally don't cost much more, if any more, than those without, and the weight difference is almost negligible. You can find such a reel for $25 to $40 Canadian in most tackle stores.

The line itself is the heart and soul of any fly fishing outfit. Since that's the part that you cast, it's generally the part you spend the most money on and pay the most attention to. Good flylines aren't cheap, and a basic, all-round line will probably cost the same as the reel, or even slightly more. Flylines come in floating and sinking varieties, as well as combinations where most of the line floats but the tip section sinks. To complicate matters further, sinking lines come in various forms determined by how fast they sink. If you need to get to the bottom in a swiftly flowing stream, you can buy a specially constructed fast-sinking line built for just such situations. But if you only want to get your fake bug below the surface of a lake and don't care how long it takes to get down there, you can select a slow-sinker. And of course there's an intermediate line for those who don't fit

either extreme. For one's first fly fishing outfit, keep things simple and buy a floating line. Not only will a floating line suit most freshwater fishing situations, but it is far easier to cast (you don't have to haul it from the depths first) and you can more readily see what's going on.

Most flylines are tapered, meaning the tip is smaller in diameter than the main body. The reason for this is to reduce weight at the end of the line, allowing the fly to land in the water more delicately so as to avoid spooking the fish. Weight-forward lines, which have the bulk of their mass in the front third of their length, are probably the easiest to cast, especially when you're just starting out, so that's the type to go with. Once you gain experience, you can experiment with other line styles and decide what you prefer.

Flylines were at one time made from silk and had to be thoroughly dried between fishing trips or else they would rot. Fishing stores used to sell big spoked wheels that you could wrap your line around to help it dry. And if you wanted the silk line to float, you had to grease it up prior to fishing. Talk about a lot of bother! But by the late 1960s synthetic flylines had blown old silk lines right out of the market. Virtually maintenance-free, tough, strong, and cheap to manufacture, synthetic lines are so much more practical that silk lines virtually disappeared from the market within five or six years.

Where conventional monofilament fishing line is measured in pounds of breaking strength, flylines are rated according to their weight. Flylines range from a diminutive number one line, made for small stream trout and panfish, up to a massive number twelve, suitable for the largest tuna, marlin, and sharks. Most freshwater fishing calls for lines from a three-weight (small trout and sunfish) up to an eight- or nine-weight (pike, muskie, and salmon, along with bass in heavy cover), with a six-weight being a good all-round choice. The term "weight" is used because the various sizes of line represent the actual weight of the first thirty feet (9.1 m) of it, expressed in grains. Each successive move up in size represents a twenty- to thirty-grain increase in weight. So a four-weight line, which weighs 120 grains, is smaller than a five-weight line, at 140 grains. This numerical system makes it a cinch to balance your rod, reel, and line. When you buy a six-weight line, you'll simply select a six-weight rod and a six-weight reel to go with it. The tackle manufacturers couldn't have made it much easier.

Most flylines run from thirty to thirty-five yards (27–32 m) in total length, which isn't much when you're fishing for big, active species that will take off on long runs when hooked. This is why most experienced fly fishermen first spool fifty to two hundred yards (46–183 m) of twenty- to forty-pound test Dacron backing onto the reel before spooling on the flyline, the amount depending upon the size of the reel. Flylines themselves rarely break; you'll likely snap your rod, and certainly your leader, long before the flyline itself ever gives out. Although the average flyline for freshwater fishing probably comes in at somewhere between thirty-and forty-pound breaking strength, they have unbelievable stretch. Most are constructed with some sort of braided nylon core covered by nylon or soft plastic, though a few use braided monofilament cores, and a handful of lines, used primarily for saltwater inshore fishing, are made from solid extruded nylon. Being greater in overall length and diameter, all have a far greater capacity to stretch than even the toughest tapered leader.

Because flylines are so large in diameter, and are normally made in brilliant colors to make them easier to see when casting, you will need something to go between the line and your fly, and that thing is a leader. A fly fishing leader is a whole different item from the steel leaders used in conventional fishing. Here, the objective isn't to protect your line from sharp teeth but to provide a low-visibility connection between fly and flyline. Almost all leaders today are made of monofilament or fluorocarbon, and they taper from a relatively thick diameter at the base to a thin diameter at the tip. In length, they run from seven to nine feet (2.1–2.7 m) or more. The purpose of the taper is to provide a continuous reduction in diameter from flyline to fly, allowing the energy from the cast to dissipate before the fly actually lands on the water. For instance, if you're trying to delicately present a small fly to a trout in shallow water, the last thing you want is for your line to roll over like a bullwhip and smash the fly down hard, with a huge splash. The taper in the leader allows that energy to escape, permitting the fly to land delicately, like a real insect.

Because fly leaders aren't exactly cheap, we use a short length of straight monofilament between the end of the leader and the fly itself, and this connection is called the tippet. Tippets may be from one to two feet (0.3–0.6 m) in length, and are usually formed from a piece of

Streamer flies, which work beneath the surface, are designed to imitate small fish. Other styles may imitate crayfish, or try to draw strikes by attracting the fish's attention.

monofilament that's about as light as one can get away with; that way, if something has to give, it's the cheap tippet and not the more expensive leader. For casting flies to largemouth bass in lily pads, twelve-pound monofilament would be appropriate. But for stream trout or panfish, we might use a tippet of six-pound, four-pound, or even two-pound mono. It really depends on the size of the fly and the amount of stuff the fish can wrap your line around.

Flies themselves come in thousands of different styles, called patterns. These different fly patterns fit into types. Some, called dry flies, are designed to float on the surface, while others (wet flies) are designed to sink, for a subsurface presentation. Dry flies typically imitate an adult insect that has landed on the water, while wet flies may imitate aquatic insects, insect larvae (these are called nymphs), crayfish, leeches, worms, or even small fish (normally called streamers). Countless books have been written detailing various fly patterns, yet there are probably thousands more that remain undocumented. So forget about trying to learn them all! Instead, think about the fish you're trying to catch and what they probably feed on, then get some flies that roughly resemble their food. If crayfish are common on your pet lake or creek, then get some crayfish flies. If it's early summer and you see lots of mayflies about, then buy some mayfly patterns. Grasshoppers bouncing around all over the place on the stream bank? Chances are a grasshopper fly will work like magic. Are the mosquitoes bad? There's a great clue to a hot pattern.

To get started you will want to buy a basic selection of flies that cover a variety of possible situations. This is where advice from your local fly fishing shop is absolutely invaluable. In most parts of North America you need only five or six types of flies to catch fish pretty well year-round. But the actual flies you should select vary based upon the kind of fish available to you, the types of insects found in your region, and the nature of the water where you will fish. There's no substitute for local knowledge, and that's where the pro at the fly shop can become your best friend. Avoid the temptation to buy a whole bunch of different flies. Instead, select a handful of types that are consistent local producers, and get to know how and when each one works best. This shortens the learning curve significantly.

One day you may get into tying your own flies, and that's really a lot of fun. Most people just make up their own flies as they go, naming them after friends or favorite fishing spots or even family pets. I still have a couple of Gizmo flies kicking around, named after the family cat from which I plucked the brilliant orange hair they're tied with.

Basic Fly Casting

Casting is the basic skill in fly fishing. Part of the pleasure in fly fishing comes from executing accurate casts, since mechanics play no part in it, unlike casting with conventional spinning and baitcasting tackle. You can't blame the gear when you mess up casting a fly outfit; it either works, or fails, because of your skill. Thankfully, basic casting technique is very easy to learn. Anyone can pick up the fundamentals in about a half an hour, practicing on the lawn. You don't even need water.

Fly fishing is a bit different from other forms of angling because of the simple fact that the offering you use, an artificial fly, has practically no weight to it. Whereas you use the weight of the bait or lure to cast in other forms of fishing, in fly fishing you don't have that luxury. Instead, you use a thick, heavy line and cast the weight of the line rather than the weight of the lure or bait. In other words, you cast the line and the fly just goes along for the ride. A fishing reel is instrumental in casting with other forms of angling, but in fly fishing the reel usually serves only as a place to store line and isn't involved in casting at all.

The mechanics of fly casting are pretty basic. To make a standard overhead cast you strip about thirty feet (9 m) of line off the reel with your free hand, and throw it back through the air with a sharp rearward flick of the rod. As the line passes you, its weight will begin to pull on the rod tip. Once the line straightens out behind you, more or less parallel with the ground, and the rod is under maximum tension from the weight of the line, you power the rod forward in a smooth arc. It's a hand-wrist-forearm motion, treating the rod as an extension of your hand. The rod responds by driving the line forward. If you did everything right, the line should lay out in front of you in a fairly straight line. Chances are, however, that for the first try, and probably for several tries thereafter, the line will be anything but straight—more likely looped in coils all over the place. Don't sweat it. It takes a few tries to get the timing right.

Beginning fly casters invariably make one of two mistakes: they bring the rod back too far when "loading" the line, allowing the tip to drop too close to the ground; or they don't wait long enough for the line to straighten out properly behind them before powering the rod forward. Because these two events happen behind you, out of your line of sight, they have to be learned through feel and feel alone. It doesn't take long to get the hang of it, though, and once you do begin to have some success, you'll find it's a pretty quick learning curve. Before long you'll be chucking line out there into stiff winds with no problems at all. It just takes practice.

A lot of casting problems stem from the way the angler grips the rod. You want a firm grip, but not too tight. I like to lay my thumb along the top of the grip, almost pinching the handle between thumb and forefinger, with the other fingers more or less hanging around in the background. In casting, I just point my thumb where I want the line to go.

Because the flies themselves weigh next to nothing, in fly fishing you cast the weight of the line, not the lure. Fly lines are made from a variety of materials, most of them brilliantly finished for increased visibility to facilitate casting.

Some competitive casters lay their forefinger along the top of the handle, but I find that type of grip limits the flexibility in my wrist. It might be OK for ten to twenty minutes in a casting competition, but trying to cast like that all morning leaves me with a sore wrist.

Once you've managed to get the gist of it, you might want to try putting a target of some sort on the lawn and see how often you can hit it. A dinner plate laid on the ground works well. For most people it doesn't take terribly long before they're able to land the end of their line on the dinner plate with surprising consistency. Congratulations! You're fly casting. That wasn't too difficult, was it?

Getting a little more distance depends on learning a second skill: how to shoot line. This is where your other hand comes back into play. Once you've made a cast, pull another ten to fifteen feet (3–4.6 m) of line off the reel and hold it in your hand in loose coils. Assuming you are right-handed, as you pick up the line off the ground to make your back cast, hold that loose line firmly in your left hand. As always, allow the airborne line to straighten out behind you, then power it forward with a smooth arc of the wrist. As the flyline drives towards the target, almost at the point where it straightens out in the air in front of you, release the loose line in your left hand. If your timing is right, it will sail down the rod and out to the target. As before, the line will lie in front of you, a straight line on the ground, the end of it further than it was before.

Distance is a relative matter, though, and fly fishing is a close-range style of angling. The vast majority of fish hooked on fly tackle are caught within twenty-five and thirty feet (7.6 and 9 m) of the rod tip, so don't get too caught up on trying to attain great distance in your casts. And never go for distance at the expense of accuracy. Once you can cast about thirty feet (9 m) of line and shoot out another fifteen feet (4.5 m) or so, you're ready to catch fish in most situations where fly fishing would be appropriate.

Advanced Casting Techniques

You'll find that the basic overhead cast works for most fishing situations. But the day will come where you run into a spot with a lot of overhanging trees. You won't be able to get a cast in there because your line will get caught in the branches. You would not believe how many times you'll run into this situation on your average trout stream. That's when you have to innovate and try a sidearm cast. The mechanics are essentially the same, but you cast with your rod held low and parallel to the water surface. Casting sidearm allows you to keep the line low so you can fling it under those overhanging branches. It's also a great technique to have on those days when the wind comes up. By flinging your line out low over the water, you keep it out of the wind and have fewer accuracy problems.

It is also only a matter of time before you encounter a situation where you have your back to a wall of trees or rock, making it impossible to cast in the standard or sidearm fashion. After all, to cast forward you need an equal amount of clear space behind you. If you don't have that much clearance, then it's time to use a technique called a roll cast. This is something that you can't really learn on dry land, since its success depends upon the weight of the line dragging in the water. It's dead simple, though.

You begin by lobbing out as much line as you can, and in even the worst situations that will probably be at least two rod lengths, or fifteen to twenty feet (4.6–6.1 m). With this line in the water and your rod held at about belt height, draw the rod tip up to a vertical position. The weight of the line, combined with the drag of the water, will load the rod. At this point you smoothly raise your casting hand about head-high, then smoothly and sharply roll the rod over and downward with a sharp snap of the wrist, while returning your hand to its original belt-high position. The line should literally roll over itself and flick out in front of you. Again, it takes a few tries to get the hang of it, but roll casting really is a lot easier than it sounds. To gain a little more distance, strip line off the reel and shoot it as you would when making a normal overhead cast.

You will almost never get the same distance roll casting as you would with an overhead cast, but when you consider the place where you normally use a roll cast—when fishing brushy streams—being able to cast a great distance is seldom a consideration. The only real problem with a roll cast is that it isn't easy to change direction. Viewed from above, you can realistically change direction only twenty to thirty degrees at a time. So if you're casting up- and across-stream then drifting your fly down through a run, you may have to make two or three roll casts in succession to get your fly back up to where you started. Sorry, but there's just no way around that.

Fly fishing certainly has its limitations, but it's a great deal of fun. Lessons learned while fly fishing have applications in other forms of angling too. Part of its charm is that it inevitably leads one to try more ambitious techniques and develop a greater understanding of fish and their habitat.

CHAPTER 8

Casting Techniques

Most of the fishing techniques we use today involve casting a lure or bait from a stationary point. Therefore, it is important to learn how to huck that bait or lure out there. I remain convinced that casting techniques are not something you can easily learn from a book; you have to go out and spend some time on the water, learning through trial and error. However, we can describe the basic approaches to casting, so let's take a closer look at what's involved in presenting our offering to the fish.

The standard overhead cast gives the best combination of distance and accuracy.

There are many ways to cast a lure or bait, but you will find that a handful of basic casting techniques will suffice for virtually all freshwater fishing situations. The most basic of these—the standard overhead cast—will meet most of your needs. Depending on the type of fishing you wish to do, the kinds of fish you want to catch, and the types of places you may be fishing, there are some other ways of getting your offering out to the fish, and we'll explore those too. And while on the subject of casting techniques, we should also have a look at what it is we do after we've flung our offering out there. But I'm getting ahead of myself. Let's first look at how we get that lure or bait out to where the fish are.

The Basic Overhead Cast

The standard way to cast a lure or bait with a spinning outfit is to wind the lure to within a foot or so of the end of the rod tip, pick the line off the reel with the end of your index finger, then open the reel's bail. Raise the rod overhead till it's somewhat beyond a vertical position, then in a smooth, fluid sweeping motion, power it forward. When the rod is at about a forty-five-degree angle to the ground, pointing in the direction you want the lure to go, release the line from your index finger. The weight of the lure should, in theory, send it sailing forward towards the spot you pointed it, peeling line off the reel behind it.

Some people like to imagine themselves standing in front of a giant clock face, facing the "nine" side. You move the rod backwards past vertical to a position that would be roughly equivalent to two o'clock, then sweep the rod forward and release the line when the rod reaches the ten o'clock position. You'll know when you get it right, because if you release the line too soon, the lure will fly straight up in the air and not really go anywhere. Release the line too late and the lure will slam into the water hard a short distance in front of you. If you really hold on too long, it may even sweep down and smack you in the shin. This is why it's best to take those first few casts with a practice plug or a lure with the hooks removed.

It doesn't take long to get the knack of it, though, and within a few minutes most people find they can fling the lure pretty much where they want it to go. At first, forget about getting any great distance and focus instead on developing accuracy. Distance will follow all on its own.

Casting with a baitcasting outfit employs the same basic motion, but the mechanical aspects of controlling the reel are different. You generally depress a button or bar of some sort to disengage the reel gears, then immediately place the tip of your thumb on the spool to hold it still and keep the line from unraveling. You then raise the rod overhead to that two o'clock position, as before. When you power the rod forward, this time you simply lift your thumb from the spool when the rod reaches the ten o'clock point, and the weight of the lure, combined with the energy from the rod, will send the lure sailing forward, pulling line from the reel.

The difference between the two forms of tackle lies in how line comes off the reel. Line flows off the end of a spinning reel. When the lure lands in the water, the energy hauling line from the spool stops, so the line simply stops coming off the spool. At this point you engage the reel handle to put it back into gear, and begin fishing. It's a little different with a baitcasting reel. When that lure lands in the water, it stops pulling line from the reel. However, the inertia of the reel spool rotating doesn't stop at all. The spool will continue to turn long after the lure lands in the water, pushing line off the reel in great coils. The result is a giant tangle, or backlash.

To avoid this problem, you have to learn how to feather the spool as the lure nears its target, by lightly brushing the tip of your thumb against the spool. Most modern baitcasting reels employ mechanical or magnetic brakes that try to do this automatically, but the fact remains, there is still no substitute for an educated thumb. Some of the braking devices really do work, but the trade-off is that they increase friction on the rotating spool at all times, which will rob you of distance. You're better off learning to do it with your thumb, so you don't have to rely on the brakes any more than necessary. And that, my friend, happens only with practice.

Bass tournament pro Rocky Crawford is a master at flipping in heavy cover. The only way to get a lure anywhere under heavy overhanging trees is with a soft underhand approach.

Regardless of which type of tackle you use, that basic overhead cast will be the primary means of propelling a bait or lure out to the fish. Casting overhead gives you the best combination of distance and accuracy—distance because your line moves high off the water surface in a favorable trajectory, accuracy because you simply point the rod where you want the lure to go, and need only control the distance. However, depending on the places where you fish or the species you're trying to catch, there are other ways of casting that you may wish to learn.

The Sidearm Cast

There are times when a sidearm cast can work a little better. You use the very same approach as you would when casting overhead, but the arcing motion with the rod occurs parallel to the ground, about belt-high. While this type of cast will generally not allow the distance or the accuracy of a traditional overhand cast, it is useful to know. When fishing in windy conditions, for example, the sidearm cast is useful because, by keeping your cast low to the water, you have fewer problems with the wind blowing it off course. Sidearm casts are also the best way to cope when there are overhanging trees or brush along shorelines, a common situation when fishing in streams and rivers. With a traditional overhead approach your lure will most likely get snagged in the branches.

Pitching

If you find yourself fishing in very shallow water for spooky fish, an underhand cast, sometimes called a pitch, is useful to know. Pitching a lure involves making a forward, underhand motion with your fishing rod, starting with the tip more or less pointing at the target, then sweeping it up in a circular, arcing motion, lobbing the lure forward with a pendulum-like swing. The idea here is to have the lure travel to its target very close to the water surface, rather than sail high in the air as it does with a traditional overhand cast. The benefit is that the lure lands with minimal disturbance, so you don't alert spooky fish to your presence or frighten them off with a big loud splash. Pitching is a stealth technique that can mean the difference between plenty of fish and no fish at all any time you're fishing in shallow, clear water.

You can pitch with either spinning or baitcasting gear. It's tough to get any kind of distance by pitching, but it is possible to develop incredible accuracy. When you're casting into little openings in a shallow weedbed, into small pools in a trout stream, alongside boat docks, or in any other situation where you have to hit a small, specific spot in fairly shallow water, pitching is absolutely the final answer.

Flipping

Flipping is like an extremely short-range version of pitching, and it's the only way to go when you need to make a super-quiet cast to a very precise spot. It is a close-range game—to close that you don't even take your reel out of gear. To flip a lure you use a fairly long rod, normally from seven to almost nine feet (2.1–2.7 m) in length. Pull enough line off the reel so that the lure can touch the base of the rod, then pull off another six to eight feet (1.8–2.4 m) and hold it in your other hand, your arm extended off to the side. Once you've positioned yourself very close to your target, swing your rod tip forward and up in the very same motion you would use when pitching and, at the appropriate moment, release the loose line in your hand. The lure should swing forward in that pendulum-like arc, mere inches above the water's surface. When it comes to the end of its trajectory and the end of the slack line, it should plop into the water with nary a sound.

Anglers new to flipping often wonder if the commotion caused by positioning one's boat within twelve to fifteen feet (3.7–4.6 m) of the target won't frighten the fish, rendering a precise, silent cast pointless. That's a valid question. But it's important to remember that flipping is a technique you really need only when you're fishing in very thick cover, such as a super-dense weedbed, along a cattail bank, or in tangles of sunken trees. As long as you're reasonably careful and quiet, the weeds should absorb some sound and visually conceal your approach. Flipping is not the way to catch shallow fish in clear water with open cover. In that situation you'll definitely frighten them with the boat.

Flipping is most often used when fishing for largemouth bass in dense cover, but it has applications in other types of fishing as well. I've used a flipping technique to lob worms into log-jams in very small trout creeks, concealing myself behind streamside brush; and it's one of my favorite ways to catch panfish, like perch and crappie, when they school on specific chunks of cover like cribs, sunken docks, and along weedlines. Flipping small jigs into open pockets in the weeds is a great way to catch early-season walleye, and a method that most anglers ignore. Pretty much any spot where you need to drop a bait into a very precise spot is a candidate for flipping.

Skipping

If you spend a few hours in a tackle store, it's a pretty safe bet you'll hear other anglers happily describing how they managed to overcome one type of obstacle or another, and catch a fish from a place no one else could even get a bait into. Over time you'll find yourself in situations where the standard means of chucking a lure or bait out there just won't cut it. Now you have to innovate. For example, it is very common to find fish holding in the shade of overhanging cover, such as boat docks or low-lying tree branches. Most anglers will fish the edge of this cover, which means the fish that hang around the edges either get caught or become highly

Casting is the number one approach when fishing streams. Dan Ralph used the current to his advantage, casting farther upstream than the place he actually wanted to fish. By keeping a tight line, he was able to use the current to steer his offering into the right spot, giving his bait an incredibly natural presentation. His plump rainbow trout—and his smile—says it all.

educated. But the big ones that lay way back in the shade almost never see lures. The trick to catching them is to somehow get your offering way back where they can see it. In the case of a dock, you may have to fling a lure several feet back under decking that sits only inches from the water's surface. What to do?

This is where a specialty technique called "skipping" comes into play. At one time or another we've all stood on the shore of a lake or pond and skipped stones on the surface. Skipping, in a casting sense, means trying to accomplish the same thing with a fishing lure. You execute what could only be termed an extremely low-angle sidearm cast, with the tip of the rod sweeping just an inch or two above the water's surface, throwing the lure towards the target so forcefully that when it contacts the water surface, it doesn't dig in and sink, but bounces up and skips across the surface just the same way those stones do. If you get your timing right, you can learn to propel a lure an amazing distance this way, skipping it along the water's surface and underneath overhanging docks, boathouse doors, and tree branches. Because the fish that live so far back under the cover almost never see a fishing lure, they're not terribly hard to fool, and it's common to get a bite as soon as your lure comes to a halt and begins to sink. I'm not sure if the little splashes from the skipping action attract their attention, but it would appear that might be the case, for fish often pounce on skipped lures *very* quickly.

Skipping was originally popularized by tournament bass anglers, but it has applications in a lot of different fishing situations. I've used this casting technique to catch both largemouth and smallmouth bass, as well as pike, muskie, walleye, rainbow trout, brook trout, brown trout, and even salmon. It's a great technique to have in your bag of tricks. If nothing else, it's a surefire way to impress your friends and earn some bragging rights when you use it to catch the biggest fish of the day.

OK, You've Cast!
Now What About Reeling Your Lure Back In?

The word *casting* carries two different meanings in an angler's lingo. Of course it describes the physical act of launching a lure or bait out there where the fish can find it. But it can also refer to an entire manner of fishing—casting and retrieving various lures and baits. If we reduce fishing methodology to its absolute basics, casting is one of two different ways to get your lure or bait out to the fish. The other way to do it, trolling, involves using a boat to maneuver your offering around. We'll cover trolling in the next chapter. For now, let's take a look at the art and science of casting—that is, using your rod and reel to present your offering to the fish.

I like casting. In fact, it's by far my favorite way to fish. Because I constantly have the rod and reel in my hands, I never get bored. The very act of working the tackle often proves to be immensely rewarding in itself; and making successful casts and working the baits is always enjoyable. When you're catching fish, there's the additional element of anticipation: you never know if that next cast will result in you hooking a trophy catch. And because you always have the rod and reel in your hands, as opposed to sitting in a rod holder, as is often the case when trolling, you always *feel* the fish hit.

Just as there are different ways to cast your offering, there are various ways of reeling it back in. You can retrieve it continuously, by cranking the reel non-stop at a slow, moderate, or high speed. Or you can take a stop-and-go approach, interrupting your retrieve with breaks and pauses. If that doesn't work, you can try jigging your lure up and down over the bottom. Or you can simply leave your bait alone and not reel it in at all. It's only a matter of time before you find something that the fish respond to.

The best approach on a given day depends on how active the fish are and, to a large degree, on what sort of lure or bait you're fishing with. When fishing with natural baits such as worms, minnows, crayfish, or leeches, the best retrieve is often no retrieve at all. Simply cast the bait into a likely looking spot and wait for the fish to find it. If you've scouted your location well, that shouldn't take long at all. Sometimes referred to as still fishing, this most basic casting technique probably catches more fish than any other. It's the ultimate in simplicity as you simply prop your rod up against the side of the boat or, if you're fishing from shore, in the notch of a forked stick and wait for a bite. For a more visual approach you may elect to attach a small float an appropriate distance up your line, and watch for the telltale bouncing that signals an interested fish. Either way, still fishing works because it keeps your bait in the water. I can't emphasize enough the importance of this rather obvious concept. Fish won't bite if they can't reach your bait.

It's amazing how easy it is to lose sight of the importance of keeping your bait in the water. Many years ago I was fishing for rainbow trout in a medium-sized river close to where I lived, enjoying a beautiful Sunday afternoon with a friend, Greg Elaschuk. By the end of the day Greg had caught five trout, while I had managed just two, even though we fished side by side throughout the day, using identical rigs and baits. This had happened before, and it was bugging me. Why did he consistently catch more fish than me? The more I thought about it, the more baffled I became. Greg and I went back to the same river a few days later, and this time I paid extremely close attention to everything he did. There had to be something different in our techniques.

By the end of the day I had my answer: the guy always had his line in the water! Where I reeled up and propped my rod against a tree when it came time to stop for lunch, Greg balanced a sandwich in one hand and his rod in the other. While I reeled up and then walked directly from spot to spot, Greg left his line in the water and walked with the current. By my guess he had his line in the water probably twice as long as I did. And sure enough, he once again caught about twice as many fish.

The importance of keeping one's line in the water came up again one afternoon on Lake of the Woods while pre-fishing for a tournament with Bob Izumi, the well-known host of television's *Real Fishing Show*. About the only time Bob's bait wasn't in the water was when the boat was going full-speed, traveling from one spot to the next. Otherwise, his bait was down there with the fish. One of Bob's favorite stories is how he caught a huge smallmouth bass during the tournament one year while rummaging through the cooler. He had cast his Zara Spook surface lure out and simply left it floating dead on the surface while he rummaged through the cooler. While he was digging out his lunch, Bob heard a loud splash and knew it was a fish. Sure enough, it turned out to be the biggest smallmouth of the whole trip—one he would never have caught had he not kept his line in the water.

So, still fishing works so well because it keeps your bait in the strike zone. But because still fishing is a passive approach, it works best in places where fish congregate in large numbers at very specific locations. I like to think of still fishing as the angling equivalent of putting up a roadside lemonade stand: you won't do much business unless you're in a high-traffic area. It's not a good choice when fish are scattered across a broad area, or during those times when you have to go looking for them. Ideal locations for still fishing are what some anglers refer to as high-percentage spots—those places where fish regularly congregate. Some examples might include the deep pool at the base of a waterfall or dam, off the end of a prominent point, along the edge of a dense weedbed, at the mouth of a river or creek, or in a current area, such as a lake narrows.

When you find yourself in a situation where the fish could be anywhere, it's often best to leave the worms in the bucket and try casting and retrieving with artificial lures instead. Because artificial lures cover so much ground, they're very effective when you have to go looking for fish that aren't concentrated in easily identifiable spots, or if you're trying to catch fish that may be scattered over a vast area. Whether I reel them in continuously or fish in a stop-and-go, I like to take a systematic approach when I cast with artificial lures, so that I cover as much water as possible.

Fan-casting is a term that describes a particular systematic approach to fishing. Instead of repeatedly casting straight in front of you, you also cast off to each side, with each successive cast landing a couple of feet over from the one before. Over a period of several minutes you can cover the entire 180-degree area in front of you, from your extreme left to your extreme right, and everywhere in between. Only after you have thoroughly covered this whole area do you move along a short distance (ideally about a cast-length) and start the process over. It's a very thorough way to cover a lot of water in a short period of time.

I like to take fan-casting to a three-dimensional level. If I'm fishing a bay or reef, I'll fan-cast the whole thing first with a shallow-running lure. Then I'll turn around and cover the whole area again, this time using a medium-diver. I may go back and make a third run with a deep-diving lure if I still don't get any strikes. With this approach, apart from covering a lot of water horizontally, I cover it at various depths too. When I finally exhaust a spot, I know there isn't a fish anywhere within my casting range that hasn't seen my lure at least once. Which lures I go with is dictated to a degree by what kind of fish I want to catch. If I'm after big pike and muskie, I'll use appropriately sized lures. But if I'm fishing for smallmouth bass or trout, I'll scale down to something more bite-sized for them.

I make lure decisions based on the day too. If I'm fishing in fairly clear, warm water for active fish, I'll often use something that I can retrieve quickly, confident that the fish activity level and water clarity will give an interested fish plenty of opportunity to chase down my lure. But if I'm fishing in off-colored water or in cold weather conditions that leave the fish somewhat inactive, or any time the fish just aren't aggressive, I switch to something I can work more slowly, giving the fish more opportunity to find the lure and make up their mind to strike it.

The advantage of this three-dimensional approach is that it gives you a good idea of what depth the fish are holding at. An eager fish may come some distance to hit a lure. If I fish only with a shallow-running crankbait, for instance, and catch a fish, I may decide that one fish is all I'll get at that spot and move on. However, by going back over the same area with deeper-running lures, I may catch several more that simply weren't willing to move up six or eight feet to hit. If I catch six fish on a lure that dives twelve feet and only one on a lure that works just below the surface, it's a pretty safe bet that by sticking with the deep diver, I'll have a more productive day.

Pattern Fishing

Say that you begin your day by fishing for walleye in a large rocky bay with some weeds here and there. After you've experimented a bit with different lures and specific locations, you catch two walleyes in a fairly short time. What were you doing when you hooked the fish? And just as importantly, *where* were you doing it? If you caught them by slowly retrieving a perch-finished CC Shad crankbait along the edge of some weeds in about eight feet of water, then you can try the very same approach with

Sometimes a stop-and-go retrieve is better than reeling straight in. That's especially true when using suspending lures that simply hang motionless at rest.

the very same lure in other locations where you have weed edges in eight feet of water. If you catch walleye there as well, you might just have discovered a pattern. Chances are that combination of a slow retrieve with a perch-finished CC Shad lure along weed edges in eight feet of water will continue to produce walleye in other similar locations on the bay. What it also means is that you can devote the rest of your time to fishing precisely those spots with that exact lure, rather than randomly trying spot after spot or lure after lure. That way, you make the most of your time on the water. If you're not catching fish on other lures or in other locations, why waste time going to more of the same? Stick to what works and you'll have a more productive day.

The key to pattern fishing is to pay attention to as many details as possible. Beyond the basics of the type of lure, the lure color, and the nature of the location, pay attention to things such as winds, currents, and sun angle. Did you catch those walleyes on weed edges that were sheltered from the wind or on ones that had the wind blowing up onto them? Was there any current in the area? Were the fish in the shade of the weeds or were they soaking up the sun? These little details all determine whether or not you can repeat your success in other spots on the bay.

Patterns are short-term things, so what works like magic in the morning might be a total bust by mid-afternoon. But if you have similar results on successive mornings, you may have discovered a "morning pattern"— one you can repeat on other days with similar weather during that same time of year. Other patterns may be seasonal. I have an incredibly dependable smallmouth bass pattern that involves natural sand beaches, but it works only in late summer.

Pattern fishing comes down to paying attention to what's going on around you while you're fishing. When you catch a fish, run through a little mental checklist and note all the factors that could have contributed to your good luck. If you notice some of these things occurring again and again, you may be on to something.

You can also get clues if you're *not* catching anything. For instance, if you have tried a number of locations and drawn a blank by slowly retrieving those perch-finished CC Shads, that's your cue to try a different color, a different size, or a different type of lure altogether. Maybe a spinner would work better. Or a live minnow. Again, you have to be systematic in your thinking. If they're not biting the CC Shad, it doesn't make sense to try slowly retrieving another perch-colored crankbait that dives to a similar depth. Try a different color, or a lure that goes deeper or shallower, or a lure you can work faster or slower than the crankbait you were using.

You can also get some hints from the weather. Never forget that fish are cold-blooded creatures, and thus their metabolism is directly linked to the water temperature. If you're not catching fish on slowly retrieved crankbaits and it's the third week of October, chances are you aren't going to do any better if you use a lure that works even faster. If the fish are cold, they'll slow down. So you should try something that goes even slower than the crankbait, like a jig or perhaps a live bait. On the other hand, if it's the third straight week of the summer's hottest heat wave and the water's as warm as soup, that slow retrieve you started out with might be too slow to interest the fish. If they're really active because the water's so warm, chances are a quicker approach will be more likely to catch their attention.

Also pay attention to ambient water conditions. Fish in murky water need time to find a bait or lure, so slow approaches work best. The same thing applies when you're fishing at night, early or late in the day, or under overcast skies. But in sunny weather and in clear water, when fish have no trouble spotting even fast-moving lures from considerable distances, you can use a quicker retrieve with confidence.

In essence, the key to pattern fishing is to pay attention to details, and to systematically experiment. Try different types of locations, using different types of lures, retrieving them in different ways. If you're fishing with a companion, you can each try different things to speed the process along. Sometimes a consistent, steady retrieve will be what works best. Most artificial lures generate some sort of wobbling or swimming action when they're reeled in. Some of these work best when reeled in slowly, others when you bring them back at a good clip; still others perform over a range of speeds. Some lures are designed expressly for fishing in a stop-and-go style, either floating, sinking, or suspending at rest, almost taunting a following fish to come on and take a nip. Bearing in mind the fast/slow retrieve guidelines based on water temperature, experimentation will reveal what works best for you on the particular waters you fish.

The real joy in casting is that you can adapt and change your approach so quickly. It's an efficient way to fish and, because it all happens at fairly close range, it's very hands-on. Sometimes you see the fish before they hit, which is always a thrill in itself. Add in the simple joy of working the tackle effectively and it's easy to understand why casting enjoys such widespread popularity.

CHAPTER 9

Fishing Boats

Although you can fish very effectively from the bank, it's tough to beat the advantages offered by a boat. Unless you fish almost exclusively on ponds or smaller streams, chances are that sooner or later you'll wish you had some sort of boat. The most obvious advantage to fishing from a boat is the mobility it affords. Having the use of a boat allows you to reach spots you wouldn't be able to fish otherwise. How frustrating it is to stand on a dock when the fish are all jumping a few yards beyond the farthest point you can cast. A boat allows you to travel to points on the lake where fish see less fishing pressure, and to fish a number of such spots with great ease. Where a shore-bound angler is restricted to fishing spots accessible from land, and even then only within a cast-length of shore, when you're in a boat, the entire lake is your playground; no fish is ever out of reach.

When you fish in a boat, you can take all sorts of equipment with you, too, since changing locations doesn't require hefting heavy tackle boxes, minnow buckets, and other such gear. You just pick up a paddle or put the motor in gear, and you're on your way. Boats also allow you to approach your fishing spots from any angle you wish. Where anglers who cast from shore have but one way of approach, an angler in a boat can move around to take advantage of wind direction or shade cast by weeds or shoreline trees. And finally, as we will explore in the next chapter, a boat can be used to help you present your lure or bait.

Surveys by boat manufacturers confirm that among the various reasons people cite for buying a boat, fishing ranks at the top of the list. Some boats are built specifically for fishing, while others are designed for more all-round use, which of course can include wetting a line. Boats designed expressly for fishing in fresh water come in a vast array of configurations and sizes, in order to accommodate anglers who fish on different-sized water bodies, travel various distances to their fishing spots, catch a variety of types of fish, and have a range of disposable incomes.

Inflatables

Popularized by Jacques Cousteau, the inflatable Zodiac and its contemporaries actually make pretty good fishing platforms. Most inflatable boats are made from a very tough, heavy, rubberized material that resists hook punctures far better than the boats that gave rise to so many misadventures for Elmer Fudd and Daffy Duck. It's pretty difficult to puncture a modern inflatable boat with a hook, even if you use pliers to help force it in (and yes, as a matter of fact I *have* tried it). The majority of them have a multi-piece, flat floor made of wood or composite panels, and a sturdy transom that allows the mounting of a small outboard motor. The big advantage to an inflatable boat is that, at the end of the day, the whole works folds up to fit in the trunk of your car—a huge plus for apartment dwellers or anglers with small vehicles.

My introduction to fishing from an inflatable came almost twenty years ago when a good friend named Henry Baraban bought his first Zodiac. Until then, I had never given them much thought. But after a few days spent chasing bass, walleye, and even Lake Huron lake trout out of it, I became a solid convert. One of the great things about the inflatable is how quiet it is. Where the sound of a tackle box scraping across the floor of an aluminum boat can carry a long way underwater, alerting fish to your presence, the hollow rubber construction of the inflatable offers a measure of soundproofing that has to be experienced to be fully appreciated. I was also surprised to find how warm one of these boats can be: the air tubes provide a lovely layer of insulation between cold water and your butt. On the negative side, the thick gunnels cut interior space, limiting capacity. And inflatables have a bizarre buoyancy that gives them a bit of a rough, choppy ride, so expect to get wet with spray.

Also in the inflatable category is the belly boat. This ultra-small craft is essentially the inner tube from a truck tire set in a nylon casing with a seat woven into the center of it. You pull it on like a pair of pants and sit in the hole in the middle, which gives you the appearance, on land at least, of a demented ballerina in a huge, inflatable tutu. Propulsion comes from your legs: you wear swim fins and paddle around backwards. Because you rely on your own kicking to propel yourself around, belly boats are not fast, nor are they efficient for covering vast amounts of water. But for fishing in relatively confined areas, such as a bay or small lake, they're great fishing platforms. Small, low to the water, and silent, they allow you to sneak up on fish like nothing else. Because most of your weight sits under the surface, they're surprisingly stable, too. And being so low in the water, you're not blown around much by the wind.

As with an inflatable boat, the biggest advantage to a belly boat is that at the end of the day you simply pull off your swim fins, step out of the boat, and fire it in the back of the car. There's no trailer to contend with, no outboard to gas up and service, no licenses to buy. Most belly boats have large pockets that hold small tackle boxes within easy reach, a spot to hold your pop, and straps for carrying a spare rod. Mine has a big apron I pull over my lap to keep me from dropping stuff into the drink, and it's marked with a measuring tape so I can see how my catches measure up.

One little gem of knowledge I learned the hard way is that belly boats are not the best craft when it comes to fishing with multi-hook lures. One of the first fish I ever caught from a belly boat was a small pike of about four pounds (1.8 kg), which smashed a Bomber Long A minnowbait I was casting for smallmouth bass. As I began to reel the fish in, it saw the dark shadow beneath my belly boat and assumed I was some sort of floating debris. It immediately made a rush towards me, darting between my legs. The back hook of the Bomber, which was protruding from the pike's jaw, snagged on the edge of my right swim fin. And I was stuck.

Belly boats, which are little more than a truck inner tube with a nylon seat, are a supremely effective fishing craft for fishing ponds, rivers and small lakes. Most have pockets to hold tackle, bibs to keep you dry and straps to carry a spare rod.

With the thick, inflatable tube surrounding me, I couldn't reach the end of my fin to free the hook, nor could I reach the fish. So with only one fin, I had to paddle, in reverse, more than 150 yards (137 m) to a spot on shore where I could stand up and free the hooks from both the fish and my flipper. All the time, the little pike was shaking and cavorting wildly on the end of my leg. Thus I learned early in the game that it's a good idea, when fishing from a belly boat, to use lures with single hooks only.

Although it has some serious limitations, I quite like my belly boat and have caught a lot of really big fish from it. If you find you spend a lot of time fishing smaller waters, a belly boat is certainly worth a look.

Canoes

Modern canoes are truly remarkable watercraft—lightweight, quiet, and able to negotiate extremely shallow water with ease. A basic sixteen-footer (4.9 m) will handle small lakes, ponds, and smaller rivers with ease, while larger canoes of eighteen, twenty, or more feet can accommodate astonishing amounts of cargo. Freighter canoes, which feature squared-off sterns and are normally powered by a small outboard motor rather than by paddling, are a staple on many northern lakes. They're big enough to handle rough water yet still travel through the shallows easily, and they go pretty darned fast with a small, fuel-efficient outboard.

The first time I ever had the pleasure of fishing from a big freighter canoe came many years ago on a visit to Kesagami Lake in northeastern

Ontario. Kesagami is a pretty big lake—more than twenty miles (32 km) long and eight miles (13 km) across—and its proximity to James Bay, with its wild weather systems, causes it to grow a bit rough at times. I was surprised to find a fleet of sturdy, twenty-three-foot (7 m) freighter canoes lined up at the lodge dock in lieu of regular aluminum boats. By the end of my trip, however, I wouldn't have had it any other way. The big canoes didn't just handle the occasional big waves, they proved far more comfortable than a regular flat-bottomed boat would have been. I was also delighted to find that they were more than stable enough to stand up in, and that they were surprisingly quick with just a small 9.9 horsepower outboard on the stern. Because Kesagami Lake sits within the confines of a provincial park, legislation prohibits the lodge owners from using larger outboards, and I seriously doubt that those little 9.9s would push aluminum boats big enough to handle the lake anywhere near as quickly.

About the only knock against canoes, and this includes the freighters, is that they do blow about a lot in the wind. It can be tough to control a canoe when fishing in windy conditions, and that's no doubt why the most popular freshwater fishing craft is the fourteen-foot (4.3 m) aluminum boat.

Aluminum Boats

The basic fourteen-footer, as these craft are so often called, has three or four bench seats of aluminum or plywood running across the width of the craft, and a wide, flared bow to deflect spray. With a fifteen-horsepower outboard, these boats are fast, stable, versatile, and almost indestructible, offering years of service with minimal care. Thanks to automated manufacturing techniques, they're also relatively inexpensive to buy. Smaller, twelve-foot (3.7 m) versions of this boat will fit on the roof rack of most cars (hence the common nickname, *cartopper*), while larger, sixteen-foot (4.9 m) models accommodate vast amounts of gear. The basic fourteen-footer represents a happy compromise between capacity and portability, and there are millions of them plying lakes and rivers around the world.

Multi-Species Boats

Higher-end fourteen-footers may offer upgraded features, such as a flat, carpeted floor, and substitution of the regular bench seating with swiveling, upholstered chairs on aluminum pedestals for greater comfort and increased storage space. These boats are heavy enough that they require a trailer, but are much quieter and more comfortable to fish from than the standard fourteen-footer. These craft, which actually range in size from fourteen to twenty feet (4.3–6.1 m), are often called "walleye boats" or "multi-species boats" because they lend themselves so well to fishing with a variety of techniques. With a flared, semi-V hull—which means the boat bottom is formed into a V-shape rather than being left flat—they

handle rough water with ease while keeping the occupants dry and well protected from spray. Multi-species boats in the sixteen- to eighteen-foot (4.9–5.5 m) class have been the hottest-selling type of boat in North America for the past two decades, and when you take a close look at their impressive features, it is easy to understand why.

Multi-species boats are sold in two basic versions, depending upon the steering arrangement. Those that are steered by the angler sitting in the rear of the boat, operating the motor via a long cylindrical handle, are referred to as tiller boats, in reference to the tiller handle on the outboard. The other style, in which the driver sits farther forward and directs the boat with a regular steering wheel, are called console boats because of the dashboard-like console that houses the steering wheel. Both arrangements offer unique advantages.

Because there's no console eating up valuable floor space, tiller boats are extremely roomy and offer a tremendous amount of storage room.

Because the outboard motor's tiller allows the driver to control not only speed but also direction with just one hand, leaving the other hand free to hold a fishing rod, tiller boats are the model of choice for anglers who like to troll. Tiller motors are less expensive than those that depend on a steering wheel, and can be installed and removed far more quickly—and much more cheaply.

Console boats, on the other hand, position the driver much farther forward, improving visibility and weight distribution, and allowing the use of higher-powered engines. Where a given model of boat with tiller control may be Coast Guard–approved to accept an outboard of up to 80 horsepower, the very same boat in a console version might be approved for up to 150 horsepower. If you need to travel long distances to your fishing spots, that extra speed gives you an obvious advantage—especially should the sunshine turn to rain and you want to get back home in a hurry. And because moving the driver forward frees up space at the back of the boat, console boats are a better bet if you plan to do a lot of trolling with downriggers or with your rods set in a holder of some sort.

Both console and tiller boats may include a variety of wonderful options designed to make the whole experience far more comfortable and enjoyable. Plush seats with pneumatic, shock-absorbing bases put an end to those kidney-buster rides in rough water. The flat, carpeted floor not only makes standing and walking more comfortable but also reduces noise and keeps you warmer in cool conditions and cooler in the summer. An aerated livewell—basically a built-in fish tank complete with water pump—allows you to keep your catch alive and happy till you get home and sharpen that fillet knife, and is terrific for keeping minnows fresh too. Locking storage compartments provide a secure place to hide away rods and valuables, while watertight storage compartments keep cameras and spare clothes from getting soggy. You can even order your boat with a CD player or, in the case of some console versions, tilt steering.

Some boat manufacturers build their larger multi-species boats out of fiberglass, but I strongly prefer the aluminum models. Aluminum handles those unexpected bumps with rocks and stumps far better than fiberglass, and is far lighter in weight. This not only makes the boat easier to tow behind your vehicle but also allows it to go a little faster on the water, and get better fuel economy besides. Aluminum boats cost less than their fiberglass kin yet require less maintenance. To me, the choice of material is a no-brainer. And on the inside, aluminum boats are every bit as comfortable as the heavier fiberglass versions.

Bass Boats

When it comes to comfort, it's pretty tough to beat a modern bass boat. Sleek, racy, and powerful, nothing makes a statement quite like one of these metal-flake rockets. With thickly padded bucket seats, plush

Sleek, fast, and incredibly stable, bass boats are the ultimate for many anglers. Although they are heavy to tow and chew up a lot of fuel, nothing else afloat can rival them for either top-end speed or simple creature comfort.

carpeting, illuminated storage compartments, wood-trim dashboards with tilt steering, stereos, and a host of standard features, a bass boat is the Ferrari of the fishing boat world.

The first bass boats were built on the hulls of small ski boats. Modern versions, which are most often fiberglass with some sort of metal-flake finish, range from sixteen to twenty-two feet (4.9–6.7 m) in length and are very wide, giving them exceptional stability. Because they sit very low in the water and weigh anywhere from 1,500 to 3,500 pounds (680–1,600 kg), they are highly resistant to being blown off course by wind. Powered by massive outboard motors of up to three hundred horsepower, most bass boats cruise along at speeds of between sixty and ninety miles per hour (97–145 kph). There's just no denying that these are serious fishing machines. If you fish on large, fairly protected waters such as reservoirs or impoundments, regularly need to travel great distances to your spots, and never intend to troll, a bass boat may be just right for you.

However, there are many downsides to bass boats. They cost a fortune to buy ($20,000 to $50,000-plus) and even more to operate: expect that big outboard to gobble up anywhere from $60 to $150 in gas, each and every day. With the exception of the smallest models, you can't safely tow a bass boat with anything less than a full-sized truck, and they don't handle rough water nearly as well as a V-hulled multi-species boat—a major consideration if you occasionally fish on big, open lakes. They're unbeatable casting platforms but positively useless for trolling, so you're restricted in how you can fish. The insurance on a bass boat is outrageous compared with other boats, thanks to that huge, high-performance power plant. And as noted previously, those fiberglass hulls just don't get along well with rocks.

Other Boats

Other styles of boats you may see on the water include center-console types, which feature the steering wheel mounted on a console located in the middle of the floor rather than along one side of the boat. Built for offshore ocean fishing, they're popular with anglers who troll on very big water such as the Great Lakes. Personally, I don't like them, because locating the console right in the middle of the floor eats up so much space and storage room. That said, on big water they do make efficient fishing platforms.

Family boats, which might include anything from ski boats to small cabin cruisers, also get pressed into use when the fish are biting. They're better than no boat at all, but lack the versatility of an aluminum multi-species boat.

It's the Accessories That Make the Boat

Regardless of the type of boat you wind up fishing from, it's important to note that the boat itself is just the starting point. What makes it more or less useful to an angler are the accessory items you install. I like to compare a fishing boat to a computer: while you can have the best computer in the world, it won't do much for you without the appropriate software. In the case of a fishing boat it's the add-ons that give a craft its usefulness.

Electric motors

In most cases you won't rely on the electric motor as your primary means of propulsion. Rather, it is a quiet and effective tool for positioning the boat once you arrive at your fishing spot. Electric motors came into widespread use in the late 1960s and early 1970s, when anglers realized they could take advantage of the silent motor to put their boat within casting distance of spooky fish. Using a gas motor, with its noise and vibration, you alert fish to your presence; not so with an electric. And because power comes on at the touch of a button, the electric is ideal for making subtle course corrections as you drift along in a current or in the breeze.

Some anglers refer to electric motors as trolling motors, due to their effectiveness when trolling in shallow water for skittish fish. They also represent a secondary means of propulsion should something happen to your boat's gas motor. More than one angler has limped back into port with the electric after experiencing some sort of mechanical difficulty that put the big gas motor out of action.

Electric motors come in both bow- and transom-mount versions, which attach to the front or rear of the boat respectively. Transom-mount motors are the simplest and least expensive, since all they require is a clamp bracket of some sort with which you screw the motor onto the back of the boat. You steer a transom-mount electric motor with a tiller handle, just as you would a small outboard motor. Bow-mount motors, which are intended to bolt to the surface of the decking, include a hinged, folding mounting bracket that adds a bit of weight and cost. Steering may be via a tiller handle or, more commonly, a foot pedal. Depressing the pedal one way turns the boat to the right, while pushing it the other way drives the boat to the left. You control the speed by turning a big knurled knob with your foot.

The advantage of a bow-mount motor is obvious: it leaves both hands free for fishing. With the motor at the front of the boat rather than the rear, you'll also find it's easier to steer and control the boat—just as it's easier to pull a rope behind you than push it ahead. Although they may cost twice as much as comparable transom-mount models, bow-mount motors are far more user-friendly.

The power of an electric motor is measured not in horsepower but in pounds of thrust. Smaller motors, which generate anywhere from twenty-four to thirty-six pounds of thrust, are ideal for canoes, car-top boats, and small aluminum boats up to perhaps sixteen feet (5 m) or so in length. Heavier boats, or those that sit higher in the water and are more prone to be blown about by wind, tend to be better matched with a forty-two- to sixty-four-pound thrust model. Still larger electrics, which may generate in excess of a hundred pounds of thrust, are meant for heavy fiberglass bass boats.

Most electric motors operate on a 12-volt power source. Rather than hook them up to an old car battery, buy a proper marine-grade, deep-cycle battery. Marine-grade batteries use thicker plates and more robust casings, which help them absorb the occasional pounding from rough water. And because you'll be drawing the power down and then recharging it, a deep-cycle battery—designed for precisely this type of use—is what you'll need. Treat a regular car battery this way and you'll kill it in very short order.

Some electric motors rely on a 24-volt power source, which means you'll need two batteries rather than one. Without getting bogged down in detail, a 24-volt motor doesn't wear the battery down as quickly as a 12-volt motor will. Even if you hook two batteries to your 12-volt motor, the 24-volt model will still go longer on a battery charge because it draws fewer amps. If you tend to go out and fish for a few hours and then head back in, a 12-volt motor will probably work just fine; but if you like to stay out there all day, or if you have a larger boat, a 24-volt motor is the only way to go. If you've splurged on a big bass boat or a really big multi-species rig, you can even find 36-volt motors that can run all weekend on a single charge of their three batteries.

I don't consider any fishing boat complete without an electric. A basic transom-mount, 12-volt motor can be found for about $150, and you can buy a top-of-the-line, 24-volt bow-mount version for about $600 (Canadian). Considering it's an item you'll use every time you go fishing, and that with reasonable care will last as long as the boat, the electric motor is a great investment.

Depth finders

Just as an electric motor is pretty much a must-have item, so too is a depth finder. Please note that I refer to this item as a depth finder, not a fish finder. True, these consumer sonar devices will show fish on their little LCD screens, but in most cases their real value is in showing the water depth and the lay of the bottom.

A depth finder works by shooting out an acoustic beam, then determining how long it takes for that beam to hit something (such as the bottom of the lake) and come bouncing back to the boat. It then calculates the elapsed time and comes up with the precise distance, which it displays as the water depth. The depth finder shoots out these little signals several times per second. As long as the time it takes for the beam to return remains more or less constant, the depth finder will display the bottom as being flat. Drive the boat over a drop-off and the greater depth will increase the amount of time it takes for the signal to return to the boat; the depth finder will then show a depth increase on its screen. Pass over a shoal and, as the depth decreases, so too does the time it takes for that signal to hit bottom and return; accordingly, the image on the screen shows a reduction in depth. It's actually quite cool how it works.

This acoustic beam is somewhat like a flashlight beam. If anything interrupts part of the beam on its way down—something suspended in the water like, say, a fish—that portion of the beam bounces back first and is shown on the screen at the appropriate depth. Suspended matter like plankton or algae shows as scratchy patches. Schools of baitfish look like bigger fish but appear hollow—the result of the depth finder's audio signal bouncing around between the individual minnows.

Interestingly, a big mark on the screen doesn't necessarily mean a big fish. The size of a fish onscreen is dependent on the strength of the echoed audio signal. A small fish that happens to be swimming in the same direction as the boat will pass through that flashlight-like beam for a fairly long time, and will thus register as a strong, solid mark on the screen. But a very big fish that's swimming the opposite way may pass through the beam for just a moment and register as a tiny blip—if it shows up at all. So you can't always go by what you see. In the same way, it's impossible to identify species by looking at a depth finder screen. You can make a good educated guess, based on the kinds of fish in the lake and the area where you see them, but you can't tell for sure based on how the signals appear onscreen.

However, the depth finder will give you a very good idea of what the bottom is like. A thick, dark, solid bottom is the result of a solidly reflected echo, indicating a hard, solid material like rock. A thin, lightly shaded, patchy bottom comes when part of the echo is absorbed by the bottom rather than bouncing off it, which indicates a soft bottom of muck, decaying vegetation, marl, or loose sand. This is valuable information. Lake trout, for instance, are almost never found on mud bottoms, so if that's what's showing on your depth finder, you're probably better off trying another spot. Depth finders also betray the presence of weeds, sunken trees, wrecked boats, old pilings or bridge abutments, and all sorts of things that can attract fish. If you're fishing in a reservoir, you can often find the old creek channel as well as things like roads, fences, and even buildings that disappeared when the reservoir was flooded.

If you use a depth finder as an aid to finding fishing spots, you'll have a practical tool. They're relatively cheap as electronic gadgets go: a good one is about $150 (Canadian), and you can buy one with exceptional detail and features for about $500.

GPS

GPS, or Global Positioning System, is a satellite-based navigation system that gained worldwide attention during the Gulf War. GPS involves a compact device that receives signals from satellites. By comparing the signals from several satellites and doing some fancy math, it can reveal your exact position anywhere in the world to within about fifty feet (15 m), at any time of day, in any weather imaginable. From a safety perspective I think a GPS should be standard equipment on any boat.

Most GPS units sold today have a memory that allows you to program in the position of various items, which it refers to as waypoints. Waypoint number one might be your own dock, so that no matter how thick the fog becomes or how many islands you wander around, you can always find your way home. Better units include a device called a plotter, which displays your position on a little map. As you drive along, your position on the map changes in real time, so you know when to turn left or right or when you've missed your turn altogether.

GPS also offers some practical benefits for an angler. Should you discover an unmarked shoal that's crawling with fish, you can punch its position into your GPS's memory so that you can return later and find it again. Or if it's a treacherous shoal you've discovered, you can avoid it entirely in future.

While you can buy small, hand-held GPS units that you can take with you wherever you go, I like the larger ones that bolt onto the dash permanently, like a depth finder. Some of these full-sized machines are compatible with electronic maps that you buy in cartridge form. It's like plugging another new game into your Nintendo system. If you like to fish on Lake Erie, then you buy the electronic map of Lake Erie and plug it into your GPS. You can then navigate with unparalleled accuracy. These little maps, which are sold under the trade name C-Map, cost about $200 a crack but are worth every penny for their incredible detail.

GPS units vary widely in price, depending on their features. It's possible to buy combination units that include a depth finder, in which case you get both functions in one machine and save some money. Unless you fish only on small lakes and ponds, buy a GPS. Like a life jacket, you have to use it only once to appreciate having it.

Freighter canoes are widely used in the far north. Able to handle big waves while carrying a massive amount of gear, they still move quickly with even a small outboard. James Mouryas appreciates their stability too. He can lean way over the side to extract a big pike from the cradle with no fear of tipping the boat.

Other boat gear

If you like to troll, you may wish to invest in some high-quality rod holders. Clutching your rod all day can be quite a strain on the wrist, particularly if you're fishing for big species like pike or muskie with large water-resistant lures. Besides, being able to pop your rod into a holder allows you to grab a sandwich or sip a pop yet still keep your line in the water. You can always tuck the rod between your legs—but I've yet to see a better way of losing a rod when you get an unexpected strike.

You may also wish to install a downrigger. This is little more than a winch with a depth counter on it, used when trolling to lower and raise a big heavy weight to any depth with unmatched precision. You lob your lure out behind the boat, then attach your fishing line to the weight with a small, clothespin-like release clip. If you have determined with your depth finder that the fish are suspended sixty-eight feet (21 m) down, you simply disengage the reel gears and lower the downrigger's weight till the depth gauge reads sixty-eight feet. As the weight descends, it takes your line and lure with it. Presto—your lure is now precisely sixty-eight feet below the surface. Your rod goes into a rod holder, and you crank up any slack line so the rod sits with the tip bent over.

When a fish hits the lure, it pulls the line clear of the line release, allowing you to fight the fish with no additional weight or drag on your line—it's just you and the fish. The downrigger weight gets cranked back up to the boat so it's out of the way while you fight the fish and have the time of your life. You can see the hit because the rod tip will either fly up in the air or slam down and buck wildly, depending on which direction the fish was swimming when it hit the lure.

Downriggers can be found either with manual cranks or with little electric motors that raise and lower the weight at the touch of a button.

Most attach to the boat permanently with a quick-release mounting plate of some sort, but others attach with a clamp arrangement. The clamp models are perfect for anglers who often fish from rental boats.

About the only downside to downriggers is the cost ($100 to $1,000 dollars, depending on features) and the fact that they eat up a bit of space at the back of the boat. For catching fish that suspend off bottom, however, they're absolutely unbeatable, and a worthwhile accessory item if you fish on bigger waters where you will sometimes find yourself trolling deeper than ten to fifteen feet (3–4.5 m). Buy one downrigger for each angler you expect to have on board.

The legal requirements for safety gear vary from one jurisdiction to another, so be sure to check to ensure your boat has all the stuff the law demands. This should include a proper-fitting life jacket for everyone on board, a horn or some sort of signaling device, a throwable rope should someone fall overboard, and some means of communication. Where coverage permits, many anglers take their cellular phone with them on the water as a safety precaution. Other anglers use a VHF radio. Flares of some sort should also be in your safety kit; if you're stuck and can't get anyone on the radio, fire a flare and someone will see it.

At least two good-quality anchors are recommended on any fishing boat. Not only is an anchor a legal requirement, but it's useful for fishing, too. When fish concentrate in specific locations, anchoring can be the best approach. I like to have two anchors rather than just one. By being able to anchor both ends of the boat, you avoid the problem of the craft swinging around in the wind, which gives you a more precise means of staying in position. Anchors vary, but regardless of which sort you select, make sure you have more than enough rope: each anchor should have at least a hundred feet (30 m). If you plan to anchor in spots where waves or wakes from passing boats will leave you bouncing up and down, then install about four feet (1.2 m) of heavy chain between the anchor and the rope. Called a rode, this link absorbs some of the impact of the boat bouncing up and down, giving you a smoother ride and reducing stress on the rope and the boat cleats you've tied it to.

Finally, don't forget a tool kit! It's amazing how often you'll discover you need one thing or another. A small plastic box with a couple of screwdrivers, a pair of pliers, an adjustable wrench, a small socket set, some electrical tape, and a good sharp knife comes in awfully handy. Toss in some spare bulbs for the trailer lights, along with a pack of spare fuses while you're at it. A spare propeller for your motor and an appropriately sized prop wrench are other good things to have, especially if you run the boat in rocky areas.

CHAPTER 10

Trolling Techniques

The greatest advantage to fishing from a boat is that it affords far more mobility than is possible when fishing from the bank. You can approach a spot and fish it from any angle you want, rather than being confined to always fishing from the shoreline side. Boats allow you to reach spots beyond casting range of shore, and to access places that are simply out of reach to shore-bound anglers. They also

Trolling very slowly with jigs is a seldom-used technique that catches big fish. This trophy northern pike hit a slowly trolled tube jig worked along a drop-off.

represent an opportunity to get away from the crowd and find fish in areas that see substantially less fishing pressure than the readily accessible spots along the shoreline.

The second great advantage to fishing from a boat is that it allows you to troll, which is a fancy way of saying you use the boat as a vehicle to present your lure or bait to the fish. But there's a whole lot more to trolling than simply tossing your lure behind the boat and going for a drive. Effective trolling relies on the angler taking a methodical approach to working specific areas, trying different depths and speeds to locate fish that can be difficult to catch by any other technique. Trolling also allows you to cover vast amounts of water in a very short period of time, making it the best approach when you're trying to catch fish that can be spread over a broad area. Trolling is also often the best approach when you're targeting fish that are not relating to cover or structure on bottom, but are suspended in mid-water. And it's an effective technique when fish are relating to structure or cover that's linear in profile, such as a rock bluff, a long drop-off, a weed edge, or a big flat point.

I took a week off while working on this book to visit a small lake northeast of Cochrane, Ontario, with a good friend, Joe Cutajar. Unknown Lake is about three miles (4.8 km) long and completely rimmed with bulrush. It's a bean-shaped lake without many prominent features like points or islands—just continuous, straight, bulrush-studded shorelines. Talk about a situation that's tailor-made for trolling. And that's precisely what we did. We experimented with different lures that would attain various depths, and tried trolling at different distances from shore, till we got onto a winning pattern. That thick bulrush grew on a shallow shelf that dropped rather rapidly into much deeper water. Combing this drop-off, Joe could do no wrong trolling a number five Mepps spinner with a gleaming silver blade, while I scored big on a gold-and-black Rebel Spoonbill minnow, which worked just a bit deeper. Both these baits worked near enough to bottom that we managed to land a number of medium-sized pike, and literally dozens of walleye, every day of our trip. We also caught fish by casting and jigging, but there was no question that trolling was the ticket on this little lake, where fish simply wandered the shorelines in search of food. In the absence of obvious features to concentrate the fish, we had to go looking for them, and trolling allowed us to cover a great deal of water in a very short time.

Trolling also shines when fish are found in water that's deeper than twelve to fifteen feet (3.7–4.6 m), since it allows you to keep a lure down at the fish's level for a greater period of time than when you're casting. Even crankbaits designed to operate at great depths reach those levels only for a short time on each cast. If you make a hundred-foot (30 m) cast, the first thirty feet (9.1 m) of your retrieve may be spent simply waiting for the lure to dive down to its working depth. And by the time it's halfway back to the boat, the pressure of your rod and fishing line begins pulling it back to the surface. So on that long hundred-foot cast, your deep-diving crankbait may have achieved its maximum depth for only twenty or thirty feet (6–9 m). Not so when trolling. Once your lure dives down to its working depth, it stays there till you reel it in or it gets hit by a fish. Trolling is simply more efficient because you spend more time with your lure in front of the fish.

Just as there are different ways of working a lure when casting, there are different approaches to trolling, based primarily on how deep you're fishing. I like to think of trolling as a shallow, mid-depth, or deep affair, based not on the water depth but on how deep I present the lure. So let's take a more in-depth look at trolling based on this premise of shallow, mid-depth, and deep presentations.

Shallow Trolling

Shallow trolling, for our purposes, means trolling at depths of less than fifteen feet (4.6 m). I suggest this depth as a maximum because it is pretty much the maximum depth we can consistently attain with most types of lures without having to use supplemental weight.

Shallow trolling is a surprisingly visual game, which may seem odd when you're towing your lure behind a boat, hoping for a bite from an unseen fish. But there's a big difference between randomly driving around and consciously working what I call high-percentage spots. The angler who randomly wanders catches fish by luck. The angler who works key locations catches fish—usually more and bigger fish, too—because he or she is going about it systematically.

Back to my trip to Unknown Lake Joe Cutajar and I knew the shorelines would attract fish, so we methodically experimented to determine which depth the fish were using and how far from shore they were. To the casual observer we may have appeared simply to be driving along the edge of the lake. But by paying attention to details such as depth and distance from shore, we were able to repeat our approach after we caught a fish, and were most often rewarded with more bites. We established a pattern.

Good shallow-water trolling situations would include the following: when fish are scattered along the edge of a piece of hard structure, such as a bluff, a steep drop-off, a ridge or trench on the bottom, a saddle, or perhaps an old river channel in a reservoir; when fish hold off straight-edged cover such as weedlines; or any time that fish scatter over a broad area. The latter is a common situation early in the season, before weedbeds develop, and late in the fall, after most of the weeds have died and fallen over. It is also common on far northern lakes, which may lack any appreciable amount of vegetation whatsoever. Some of the expansive lakes in Canadian Shield country fit into this category. These deep, rocky fishbowls lack the fertility of more southern waters, so fish tend to scatter and spread out rather than gather at predictable locations.

Successful trolling, then, comes down to visualizing what the lake bed looks like, deciding the most likely spots for the fish to sit, then systematically covering water. If you're trolling along a reef or shoal, try to visualize in your mind where the shoal begins and ends based upon visual landmarks, a navigational chart, or the information on your depth finder. One trick of the pros is to use small marker buoys to outline the position of the shoal, then systematically troll through the area, covering all the water between the markers. This tactic works well for marking weed edges too. You can buy a package of three markers, complete with a little stand for storing them in your boat, for just a few bucks.

Perhaps the biggest question about shallow-water trolling is how far to run the lure behind the boat. I have come to believe that fish are far less frightened of boats than many anglers suspect. Common sense would suggest that the shadow of a big boat passing overhead would terrify fish, especially when combined with the churning sound of an outboard motor. But fish soon become accustomed to the sound of boat engines, just as people who live near airports become oblivious to the roar of jets overhead. That being the case, you can often run your lure only a short distance behind the boat and catch fish. Operating this way allows greater precision when negotiating turns or when working around structure, and the shorter line provides better feel of the lure, so you can more quickly detect when it fouls in weeds or when you get a bite from a fish. Because monofilament line stretches, it's not easy to determine what's going on when your lure is a hundred feet behind the boat. This is why so many anglers use non-stretch braided lines on their trolling outfits: they enjoy far better feel. I usually begin trolling by casting my lure behind the boat, using that distance as a starting point. If I don't get any bites, I may let out more line to run the lure farther from the boat. Sometimes, especially in very clear lakes, the additional distance can make a difference.

When more than one angler is fishing from the same boat, or when fishing in places where you're allowed to use more than one line per person, it's important that all the lures used are compatible at the same speed. All fishing lures work best when pulled through the water at a particular speed. A lure like a Flatfish, for example, works best at very slow speeds, and will actually flip over and not work at all if you move it too quickly. Other baits, such as a Rebel Fastrack Minnow, are designed to work best at a relatively quick speed, while still others, like a Mepps spinner, perform well over a broad range of speeds. The point is that all lures in the water should work well within the same speed range. If one of the lures being used is trolled too fast or too slow, it won't catch fish.

When trolling fairly shallow water, you may sometimes find that your boat simply goes too fast, especially when fishing in current areas or in windy conditions. That's when a technique called backtrolling can save the day. Backtrolling is simply the act of driving with the boat in reverse—going backwards—rather than in forward gear as normal. Almost all motors operate at slower speed in reverse gear. As well, you'll have the additional resistance resulting from directing the boat through the water by the flat stern-end first instead of the hydrodynamic bow. And going backwards increases drag, further decreasing boat speed.

Apart from slowing the boat, backtrolling offers more control when you're trying to follow precise trolling routes along weed edges or rocky points. Because it's the end of the boat with the power that travels first, you can maneuver better in tight quarters. Backtrolling is easiest in a boat with a tiller motor, but it is possible with a console boat once you get used to steering in reverse. I prefer tiller boats for backtrolling since you can control not only direction but also speed with just one hand, leaving the other hand free to hold your rod.

For backtrolling in inclement weather, you can buy Plexiglas shields, called splashguards, that mount on the back of the boat to prevent waves from breaking over the stern and entering the boat. If nothing else they'll protect you from spray, and are a worthwhile investment should you find yourself backtrolling a lot.

Trolling is the most effective means of covering large amounts of water in a short amount of time. Joe Cutajar sometimes likes to backtroll, which means putting the boat in reverse gear and directing it stern-first. This not only slows your boat speed but also allows far more precise maneuvering around cover like weed edges.

Mid-Depth Trolling

The basics of trolling in shallow water also apply to fishing the mid-depths, which for our purposes means water from fifteen to thirty-five feet (4.6–10.7 m). The exception is that you will need to add supplemental weight to your line, in order for your lure or bait to reach the bottom in these greater depths.

There are a variety of different styles of weights used in trolling. Regular split shot sinkers pinched to the line will work, but I tend to use one of three styles designed specifically for trolling situations. By far my favorite is the bottom bouncer, which we examined in chapter 4. Looking somewhat like an L-shaped piece of wire with a weight molded onto it, a bottom bouncer is a formidable piece of gear. Its heavy weight, ranging from ¾ ounce (21 g) up to four full ounces (113 g) or more, allows it to hold bottom even at great depths and surprising speeds. Its slender profile adds little drag on the line, and its wire stem slides over rocks and snags without hanging up. It's simple but, for fishing very near the bottom, exceptionally effective.

You rig a bottom bouncer by tying it directly to the end of your line. You then take four to five feet (1.2–1.5 m) of spare monofilament and use

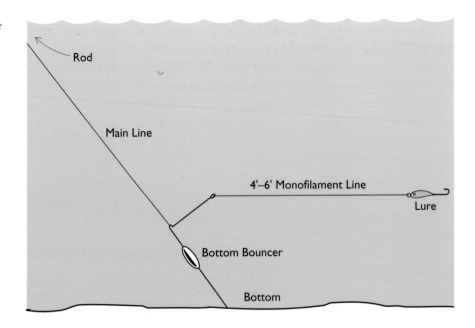

Bottom bouncer rigs are tremendously effective when you want to troll right near the bottom.

Rod

Main Line

4'–6' Monofilament Line

Lure

Bottom Bouncer

Bottom

that to attach your lure, tying on to the snap-swivel provided on the end of the short wire arm at the top of the bouncer. Rather than cast it out behind the boat, you simply lower it to the bottom. I like to maintain a fairly steep angle in the line between my rod tip and the bouncer; doing so keeps it vertical over bottom, improving its snag resistance. If you have a tough time maintaining a steep angle, replace the bottom bouncer with a heavier one.

The alternative to the bottom bouncer is the venerable Wolf River rig,

Wolf River rigs remain the best choice when fish suspend a short distance above bottom. By experimenting with the amount of line between the three-way swivel and the weight, you can quickly determine just how far off bottom the fish are holding. For deep trolling, using wire line to the swivel, with monofilament to the lure and the weight, makes a highly effective combination.

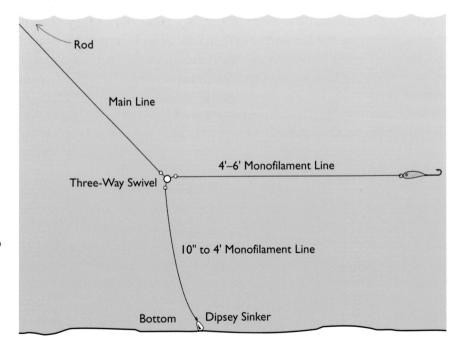

Rod

Main Line

4'–6' Monofilament Line

Three-Way Swivel

10" to 4' Monofilament Line

Bottom

Dipsey Sinker

which involves a big dipsey sinker, some spare line, and a three-way swivel. You tie your fishing line to one eye on the swivel, and use a three- to five-foot (0.9–1.5 m) length of spare line to attach a lure or bait to swivel eye number two. To the third eye of the swivel you tie a twelve- to twenty-four-inch (30–60 cm) length of monofilament, then tie on the dipsey sinker. The idea here is that the heavy weight hangs below the lure, so that if something gets stuck on bottom, it will be the cheap sinker and not the expensive bait. Most anglers use much lighter line for attaching the sinker, with the idea that it will break before the line to the lure will. For example, if you're using fourteen-pound line to the swivel and to your lure, you would tie the sinker on with something lighter, like eight-pound monofilament.

I'm not sure exactly where the name Wolf River rig comes from. There are dozens of rivers in North America named Wolf, and no one seems to know which gave rise to this useful bit of rigging. Not that it's terribly important to know. The good part is that it's a simple, inexpensive, and extremely effective way to set up for trolling in moderate to deep water. One advantage of the Wolf River rig over a bottom bouncer is that you can easily control the height that your lure runs over bottom. If the fish are six or seven feet (1.8–2.1 m) above bottom, you can simply run six feet (1.8 m) of line between the swivel and the sinker. Whereas the bottom bouncer shines for fish located right on bottom, the Wolf River rig comes into its own when you're trying for fish suspended some distance above it.

The third variety of sinker I use for trolling in moderate depths is called a snap weight. A truly brilliant idea, snap weights were developed by Great Lakes walleye anglers, who needed heavy sinkers that could be attached and removed from the line very quickly and easily. These anglers, fishing in clear water, often attach their sinkers a dozen feet (3.7 m) or more up the line from the lure. Obviously, that represents a problem with a conventional style of sinker, since the weight won't pass through the rod guides, leaving the angler basically stuck with a fish on the line and several feet of line separating him or her from it. Hence the idea of a removable weight that clips onto the line with a little clamp

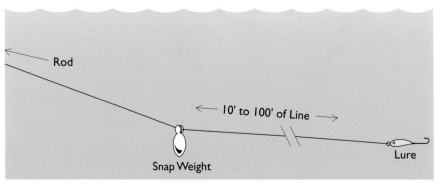

A snap weight looks like a little lead cigar with a clothespeg on top. You simply pay out line behind the boat as far as you like, then snap the weight in place on your line. When reeling the fish in, you simply reel up till you can reach the weight with your free hand, then remove it and continue landing the fish.

139

arrangement, very much like a clothespin. Once a fish is hooked, the angler reels in normally till the weight comes within reach. Simply pinching the little tabs releases the weight from the line, and the angler can continue reeling in the fish.

Snap weights come in a wide range of sizes suitable for use with a huge variety of lures and baits that are fished at moderate depths. Snap weights aren't a good idea when fishing on bottom in water with a lot of snags, since they can (and do) snap right off the line when you get stuck. But for fishing in open water, particularly for fish that are suspended in the water rather than sitting right on bottom, they're very tough to beat.

Deep Trolling

Sometimes you just have to go deep for the big ones, particularly when angling for fish that like cold water, such as lunker pike, lake trout, and bruiser salmon. Through most of the year the coldest water is at the bottom of the lake, most often in extreme depths; for our purposes that can be anything beyond about thirty-five feet (11 m). That's when specialty approaches come into play.

The simplest way to troll near bottom in deep water is to use an oversized version of the Wolf River rig, with a massive sinker of six ounces (170 g) or more. This huge weight will require the use of a fairly heavy rod, reel, and line, with a heavy-action baitcasting rig and twenty-pound monofilament a *minimum*. Deep trolling with heavy weights is no place for light tackle—that is, unless you enjoy losing gear to the rocks on bottom.

The biggest bugaboo about trolling deep is that monofilament line tends to be so stretchy that you lose feel. It can be tough enough determining when you have a fish, let alone having to monitor the action of your lure. Dacron line, or some of the so-called superbraids like Fireline, don't stretch at all, giving the angler far better feel and control. But for deep work it's still tough to beat wire. A good-quality wire line used on a heavy-action baitcasting outfit, with a Wolf River rig, gives unmatched precision when you need to probe the depths.

Wire trolling line comes in both solid and multi-strand versions. I prefer the multi-strand variety as I find it far less prone to kink. Although solid, single-strand wire does offer very low diameter, which enables it to slice through the water more easily, the stuff is so springy and prone to kink that it's frustrating to fish with. Multi-strand, or twisted, wire is far more user-friendly.

Not only does wire line not stretch, but its weight alone helps sink the lure quickly, while its small diameter allows it to cut through water easily rather than be buoyed up by the resistance. You don't cast wire (ever!) but simply lower the lure into the water and, with your thumb on the reel spool to prevent an overrun, lower the rig to the bottom. Attach the wire

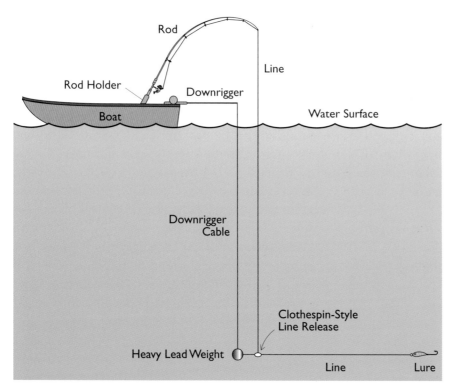

Rod

Line

Rod Holder

Downrigger

Boat

Water Surface

Downrigger
Cable

Clothespin-Style
Line Release

Heavy Lead Weight

Line

Lure

Downriggers are little more than small, hand-cranked or motorized winches with a heavy weight on the end of a long steel cable. The weight, called a cannonball, has a clothespeg-like line clip on it. You pay out line behind the boat then once your lure is back far enough, pinch the line into the clip. If you want the lure to work fifty feet (15 m) down, you simply lower the downrigger weight till its depth counter reads fifty feet (15 m). Voila! Your lure is at precisely fifty feet (15 m). When a fish bites the lure, it pulls the line free of the weight clip and you fight the fish normally. The downrigger cable is retrieved to get it out of the way and have it ready to go again after you boat the fish.

directly to the three-way swivel, then complete the rest of the Wolf River rig with monofilament so that in the event you do get snagged on bottom, you won't become permanently anchored.

With practice, you can develop a feel for wire line that allows you to tell with uncanny accuracy just what's going on, even when trolling at tremendous depths. You can work your lure along the face of shoals and reefs, know immediately if it fouls on weeds or a stick, and feel the hit of the fish like never before. Where in the past anglers fished wire on heavy rods equipped with massive single-action reels, today's wire is so well made you can use it on a heavy-action baitcasting outfit, which is far more enjoyable to handle and allows smaller fish a fighting chance. Although some anglers claim the wire abrades the rod guides, I've used it this way for some time and never experienced that problem.

Though wire line with a Wolf River rig is the undisputed king for fishing near bottom in deep water, it's not so good when you're targeting fish that are suspended. With wire you never really know exactly how deep you are, so when you mark fish on your depth finder that are seventy-four feet (23 m) down and about thirty feet (9 m) above bottom, you can't be sure they can even see your lure. For all you know, you could be trolling twenty feet (6 m) deeper or shallower than where the fish are. This is precisely where downriggers, described in the previous chapter, come into play. You let out line so your lure is a suitable distance behind the boat, then clip your line to a release pin on the downrigger weight. If you

John Hagerman finds trolling unbeatable when walleye invade shallow flats at night. With the fish widely spread out, he goes looking for them.

should mark fish on your depth finder at seventy-four feet (23 m), you can use the downrigger's depth counter to lower the weight, and your lure, to precisely that depth. They're wonderful devices, and utterly unmatched for controlled-depth trolling.

You can use any sort of rod and reel in conjunction with a downrigger, but most anglers go with long, whippy trolling rods (often sold as downrigger rods) with wide-spool baitcasting reels. Spooled with monofilament line in the seventeen- to twenty-pound class, they're wonderfully efficient outfits capable of handling the largest salmon, muskie, and lake trout. However, you can use an ultralight rod if you want a challenge, troll for giant salmon and lake trout with gossamer four-pound line, or even use a fly rod. Once you've set your lure at the correct depth, you wind up the slack line to the point where your rod is bent over in an arc, and place it in a rod holder. When you get a hit, the rod tip will either fly up in the air or slam down and throb wildly, giving you a visual signal of the hit. You then pull the rod out of the holder and fight the fish. It couldn't be easier.

A more portable, but less precise, method of presenting lures to suspended fish is to use a device called an in-line planer. Sold under the trade names Pink Lady, Dipsey Diver, Deep Six, and Yellow Bird, these plastic and metal products attach to your fishing line several feet up from the lure. They're sort of like a cross between a heavy weight and a little water ski. The weight of the planer takes the lure beneath the surface, where water pressure pushes it deep, hauling the lure in tow. If you hold your hand out the car window as you rush down the freeway, you can feel the air pressure pushing your palm up, down, or to one side, and that's precisely how planers work.

About the only knock against planers is that they're nowhere near as precise as a downrigger. Lacking a depth gauge, you really don't know if your offering is fifty feet down or seventy. So, you have to experiment by letting out more or less line till you hook a fish. Unless you use a special trolling reel with a built-in line counter that measures how much line you've let out, you're back to the drawing board after you land the fish. On the positive side, a planer costs only about $10 and fits in your tackle box. They're great for canoe trips or fly-ins to remote lakes, where you need to travel light.

You've Hooked a Fish! Now What?

S o you've studied the fish you want to catch, selected a good spot, rigged up with the correct type of tackle, and made a sensible approach. And wonder of wonders, you've managed to hook a fish! Now what? This is where we appreciate having spent the time to pick out an appropriate rod and reel, and become grateful for having purchased a good-quality line and not gone with that cheap stuff from the bargain bin—especially if it is a big fish.

Back in the chapter on rods and reels I touched upon a reel feature called the drag. Once again, the drag is the name for a slipping clutch mechanism built into fishing reels. When you hook a fish and it tries to swim away, it will put force on the line and inevitably something will have to give: either the line breaks or the hook pulls out. The drag prevents either of these things from happening by yielding line under pressure. The drag has a range of operation, normally adjusted with a knob on the end of the spool or at the back of the reel on spinning reels, or with a little wheel at the base of the handle if you're using a baitcasting reel. The idea is to adjust the drag so that the reel will yield line under pressure, setting it so the fish has to exert some effort to get the line out yet not so much that the drag is too firm and there's a risk of breaking the line.

Think of it this way: if you lightly pinch a spool of thread between thumb and forefinger and then pull thread off the spool with your other hand, the spool will slowly revolve, yielding line. Pinch the spool harder and it will take more effort to pull thread from it. Pinch too hard and the spool no longer gives up any thread. You want that happy medium.

Normally, you adjust the drag before putting your bait in the water, because by the time you hook a fish, you have enough going on to keep you busy without having to fiddle with the little knob, wondering if you

got it right. Whether you're using a spinning outfit or a baitcasting rig, taking the time to correctly adjust your drag prior to fishing is essential, particularly when targeting species like pike, muskie, trout, or salmon, which tend to run and peel large amounts of line from the reel.

With time and experience you will be able to tell if your drag is set correctly simply by pulling line from the reel by hand and gauging the tension. But until you get to that point, there's another way to do it that works extremely well. Simply tie the line to a large stationary object (a picnic table, the car bumper, a friend's wrist—anything that won't move under pressure will do), then lift the rod. The top half of the rod should bend over into a nice smooth arc before the reel gives up any line. If it lets out line freely before you reach that point, it's too loose, and the fish will be able to peel line from the reel without much effort; that's your cue to tighten it down a little. On the other hand, if your rod develops a serious bend and the reel still won't let out line, the drag is too tight, so you should ease it off a touch. You want the reel to yield line only after the rod develops a reasonable bend. Once you get the drag set more or less right, leave it alone and don't fiddle with it when you fight a fish. With the drag set correctly, any fish that bites your offering is going to have a very difficult time escaping, and there's no need for further adjustment.

One mistake a lot of anglers make is to try and adjust the drag during a battle with a big fish. When a trophy tears off for the horizon and peels line from your reel, the instinctive reaction is to tighten the drag and try to stop it. This is a bad move, almost always resulting in line breakage. If you really believe you need to put more pressure on the fish, use leverage on your rod to make the fish work for every yard of line it takes out. Hold your rod high and let its spring action do the work.

I remember, while working at a sportsman's show one winter, a discussion I had with an angler who took exception to an article I had written for a local fishing magazine the previous year, in which I described landing chinook salmon of up to thirty pounds (14 kg) on six-pound monofilament line. This gentleman tried it and got spooled: he hooked a fish that then took off and didn't stop, cleaning out all the line on his reel. Following this experience he felt it was impossible to land a large salmon on such light line, and didn't mince words in telling me he thought I was talking through my hat. But the truth is, landing a thirty-pound chinook salmon with six-pound line is no astounding feat—provided the drag is set correctly and you use the rod to fight the fish. In fact, light-tackle saltwater anglers regularly land much larger, faster, tougher fish on six-pound monofilament, including big sailfish and marlin. The International Game Fish Association's Year 2000 record book lists a number of huge fish caught on six-pound line, topped by a massive 342-pound (155 kg) mako shark. Obviously, that isn't something that happens every day, but it does go to show what is possible with a drag that is set correctly.

When it comes to fighting the fish, the most common mistake I see anglers make is holding the rod high and cranking wildly on the reel, almost as if attempting to winch the fish up onto the bank. This works with very small fish, but it's courting disaster with anything bigger than a tiddler. In the case of spinning tackle it is also a wonderful way to twist one's line into a horrible mess, leaving it virtually unusable. Next time you try to cast, the line will erupt from the reel like a coiled spring—a Slinky having a bad hair day.

The whole point of using a fishing rod, apart from casting, is that it functions as a shock absorber when you hook a fish. If the fish is swimming away and peeling line off the reel, all you can do is hold the rod high and let it go. You won't stop it—and you'll probably break the line if you try. But since the average fishing reel holds a couple of hundred yards of the stuff, just let the fish go when it runs. Before long it will grow tired and stop. That's when you can begin using your rod and reel to haul it in.

The rod and reel work in concert. You lift the rod, using it to pull the fish closer. Once you've lifted about as high as you can, you smoothly lower the rod while simultaneously reeling in line. Don't just drop the rod and allow all kinds of slack; lower it in a controlled, even fashion so the line's never really slack at all—just not really tight either. Then, when it's almost parallel to the water, lift once again and continue to draw the fish closer.

This pump-and-reel, pump-and-reel action is what will bring the fish to hand. Fighting the fish this way never allows your line to come under sufficient tension to break it, yet it keeps the fish working the whole time, with no opportunity to rest. Should you ever get the chance to fish for big game in salt water, you'll soon learn it's the only way to land a fish that's bigger and stronger than you. Should the fish take off on another run and again peel line from the reel, just let it go, and resume lifting and reeling when it stops. It won't take long to tire it this way, and you'll soon have it in the water in front of you, probably on one side, completely tuckered out.

What you do next is determined by what you have in store for the fish. Are you going to keep it and eat it? Or are you going to take the hook out and let it go? If you're going to release the fish, the best way to handle it is to not handle it at all. Just leave it in the water and simply reach down with a pair of needle-nose pliers, grab the hook, and with a quick flick of the wrist pop it backwards and out. The fish will depart at once.

If you can't get the hook out this way or if you want to hold the fish for a quick photo, try to handle it as little as possible. Bass are easily grabbed on the lower jaw, by placing your thumb on the tongue and your forefinger beneath the jawbone. This gives you a terrific grip and, as a bonus, puts the business end of the fish facing you so you can easily get the hook out. But that's not a good idea when dealing with fish like pike, walleye, or larger trout, which have far more prominent teeth. Small to medium-sized critters can simply be grabbed across the back, by spreading your thumb and forefinger over the fish just behind the gill covers. Again, this gives you a good grip and leaves the mouth facing you for convenient hook removal.

It's important to remember that fish can't breathe when they're held out of the water for a photo or to facilitate hook removal. A few years ago a photographer friend suggested I hold my breath while holding fish for the camera. As he explained, by the time I need another breath, the fish will too. Talk about a not too subtle reminder.

If you're fishing from shore or wading in a stream, the simplest way to land a fish is to beach it. Using your rod for leverage, lead the fish into a shallow area where there's a gently sloping bank. When the fish feels the bottom underneath it, it will try to swim. Because you're using your rod to point its head towards the shore, that should push it up either high and dry or, at the very least, into shallow enough water that you can run it down and grab it before it gets away.

The best place to beach a fish is on a gently sloping bank composed of fingernail-sized, smooth rocks. Sandbanks work well too, but you'll have to be careful to avoid getting sand in the fish's gills if you intend to release it. High, steep banks or banks with debris in the water are bad choices for beaching. Steep banks make it tough to grab the fish before it has a chance to dart back into deeper water, while brushy shorelines increase the risk of getting the line or lure caught on something at a critical moment.

Large, active fish can be landed by beaching them. Simply lead the fish into shallow water and keep its head pointed toward shore. When it feels the bottom beneath it, it will try to swim. More often than not, its efforts simply push it up shallower still, where you can walk over and pick it up.

The most popular way to land fish is with a net. The idea here is not to chase the fish with it but simply to place the net in the water and have the angler use the fishing rod to lead the fish over top of it. Once the fish is centered in the net, you simply raise the net hoop a few inches above the water level and the fish isn't going anywhere. There's no need to lift the fish from the water, or swing it over the side of the boat as you sometimes see in cheesy fishing magazine pictures. Just lift the frame a few inches above the surface and the fish won't escape.

If the net has a particularly deep bag, I like to gather the end of it in my hand and pinch it against the net handle while getting into position to land the fish. That way the mesh is controlled rather than simply billowing freely in the water, where it might tangle on a hook and allow a trophy catch to escape. With the fish centered over the net, I simultaneously release the mesh and raise the net hoop clear of the water in one smooth, continuous motion, which effectively puts the fish in the bottom of the bag where it has little chance of escaping. Under no circumstances should you chase the fish with the net or attempt to net any fish tail-first, for such things will only frighten the fish further and increase its chances of escape. If it's a very big fish that doesn't fit easily into the net, try to net it headfirst, since any escape attempts it makes will only serve to push it deeper into the bag.

With the fish encased in the mesh and the hoop held clear of the water, you can then reach into the water, untangle the fish, and unhook it. Do not attempt to lift the fish clear of the water by straining on the net handle; this is the surest way I know to break a net. Unless, of course, you like having to replace equipment frequently and enjoy chasing fish around the bottom of your boat.

Landing nets come in a wide range of sizes and styles. Size is rather obvious and doesn't need further explanation; if you're after big salmon and muskie, a little trout net won't do the job. But the range of bag materials does warrant some consideration. Most nets you see use a mesh made of a coated nylon material, which feels stiff and wiry to the touch. Upon closer examination you can see the mesh is held together by a series of knots. These knots are hard on fish, and for this reason I dislike using nylon nets on fish I intend to release. They tend to split the fins and tails, making it decidedly more difficult for the fish to get around afterwards, and inviting potentially fatal infection.

Better nets are made of softer material sold under a variety of trade names, such as Kerlon. While these nets too depend on knots in their construction, they tend to be made of finer mesh that is far less likely to split fins, and the softer material is also less likely to remove slime. Of course, these better-quality nets cost more, but with minimal care they last a lifetime.

You can also buy nets with a bag made of rubber, and these are my favorite. The rubber bag is gentle on fish, and as an added bonus it's almost impossible to tangle hooks in it. When fishing is fast and the bite is on, the last thing you want to be stuck doing is untangling a multi-hook lure from a wad of wet mesh. The rubber nets work wonderfully while eliminating this problem entirely, so they're my first choice. About the only negative with rubber nets is that it's very difficult to find them in sizes large enough for pike and salmon. They do exist, but you may have to special-order one from your local tackle shop. They're a bit more expensive than mesh nets, too, but they tend to last longer.

One other type of net deserves special mention, and that is a device known as a cradle. This is quite unlike the traditional landing net. Rather than a basketball hoop–like bag and a long straight handle, a cradle consists of two wood or aluminum poles of four to five feet (1.2–1.5 m) in length, which sit parallel to each other with a fine mesh bag in between. Cradles were developed specifically for use on large pike and muskie, fish that are often so long that they suffer spinal injury when balled into a traditional bag-type net. You use a cradle the same way you would a regular net: position it in the water, lead the fish over it, then raise the frame above the water level. Many anglers have found that they also work extremely well on large salmon, trout, and walleye. As an added bonus, they take up a lot less space in the boat when they're not in use.

Occasionally one winds up with a fish that is hooked very deeply or hooked in the gills. You can buy special tools for reaching way back into a fish's mouth to disgorge a hook you can't reach with pliers. If you've caught the fish on a single hook, you may be better off simply to cut the line as close to the hook as possible and leave it in. Bronzed hooks rust quickly. The rusting action, combined with the actions of the fish's own body fluids, will dissolve the hook in a surprisingly short time. I've caught several fish that had hooks in them already, some that had been caught quite recently, others where all that remained was a little telltale scar. Unless the hook is right in gill tissue, it generally won't kill the fish.

If the fish is hooked on a big lure, you obviously don't want to leave that huge gob of wood or plastic in its mouth, which would no doubt interfere with feeding. I carry a small pair of side cutters in my tackle bag and just snip the affected hook to minimize the amount of stuff I leave behind. Besides—I want that lure back!

Fish that are to be kept and eaten are handled a bit differently. While many anglers like to put their fish on a stringer, with the intent of keeping them alive and fresh, I prefer to kill eating fish at once, especially when angling in warmer weather. Fish on stringers often expire in short order anyway, which leaves your dinner lying in the sun in what is often soupy-warm water. Apart from killing the taste, this could lead to legitimate freshness problems. I've always found it's better to kill the fish and put it on ice as quickly as possible. If I intend to take a few fish home, I'll make a point of bringing a cooler and ice for this very purpose.

The simplest way to kill a fish is to give it a good sharp whack on the head with a convenient rock or stick, or one of the little billy clubs sold in tackle stores. The idea is to kill it, not hurt it, so hit it *hard* and get it over and done with. Then, time permitting, you may wish to gut it immediately and remove the gills. I prefer to remove these soft tissues as soon as possible to maintain the freshness and prevent spoilage. Don't forget the kidney, which appears as a dark patch of congealed blood along the spine; this can be scraped out with an old spoon.

Up until the late 1970s anglers traditionally kept most if not all of the fish they caught. Not surprisingly, in many areas this practice seriously depleted fish stocks, especially in the case of slow-growing fish like lake trout and walleye. Today most anglers are more judicious about keeping fish for the table. Some people prefer to release all the fish they catch, and that's perfectly fine. Other anglers, me included, enjoy the occasional fresh fish meal, and that too is quite acceptable. The key is to be selective and keep only those fish you really will eat. Simply keeping fish so you can show them to friends or family, or to toss them in the freezer till they freezer-burn into an unrecognizable mess, is a senseless waste. Many anglers have found that some of the best eating fish are the panfish: perch, crappies, and sunfish. Highly prolific, these small, easy-to-catch species are relatively easy to fillet and supremely delicious, particularly when breaded and pan-fried. Personally, I'll take a feed of crappies or perch over a couple of bass or pike fillets any day.

I won't get into fish recipes or cooking techniques, since there are already scores of excellent cookbooks available that cover this subject in great detail. But it is appropriate to talk about preparing the fish *for* cooking, because how you prepare the fish will have a major bearing on how the final product tastes, regardless of the recipe you go with. Assuming you have already gutted the fish and kept it cool, you will first need to determine how it is to be prepared. If the fish is to be cooked whole, as is popular with trout and salmon, all it will need is a good rinse under the tap and it's pretty much ready to go. Species such as walleye, panfish, and bass are normally filleted prior to cooking, so you'll need a good-quality fillet knife and a suitably sized cutting board.

Filleting fish is easy providing you have a good sharp knife. Using a dull knife is the surest way I know to botch the job and/or slice off a finger, so take two minutes to sharpen the blade first. Then, with the fish laid flat on its side on the cutting board, its back towards you, make a vertical cut across the fish right behind the gill cover, cutting down to, but not through, the spine. In the case of smaller fish like perch, trout, and sunfish, I then hold the knife flat and slice down the length of the fish, following the spine, all the way to the tail. Repeat on the other side and you should wind up with two lovely fillets. Laying the fillets skin side down, I then remove the rib cage by gripping it between thumb and forefinger and lifting it while slowly paring it away from the flesh with the tip of the fillet knife.

You can use the same technique on larger fish with heavier ribs, such as walleye or small salmon, but cutting through those thicker bones will dull your knife in no time flat. To avoid this, make your first cut behind the gill cover as before, but then slice into the back towards the spine, inserting the knife with the sharp side of the blade towards the tail, directly behind the first slice. When you feel the knife blade reach the top of the rib cage, continue cutting along the back towards the tail as before, running the tip of the blade along the top of the rib cage rather than slicing through it. When you come to the end of the rib cage and the rear portion of the body cavity, slide the knife all the way through the fish and, as before, follow the spine to the tail. This leaves you with a fillet that is still attached at the ribs. What you do then is lift the fillet with one hand and use the tip of the blade to pare the fillet off the ribs with the other. It takes a little longer this way, but it saves wear and tear on the blade. Some anglers prefer to stick with the first method but use an electric knife literally to saw through the ribs. It works like magic! I've come to prefer this method to any other; it's not only much faster, but wastes less meat and results in a neater-looking fillet.

Removing the skin from the fillets is easy. Simply lay the fillet skin side down on the cutting board and cut through the flesh at the tail to, but not through, the skin. Holding a regular fillet knife (*not* the electric one) right to the board and on about a forty-five-degree angle, keep the knife still and, with a firm grip on the skin, slowly walk it backwards against the blade. Get the motion right and it peels off like a strip of masking tape.

In the case of very large species like salmon, you may wish to cut the forward part of the fish into steaks. Simply lay it on a cutting board, and with a very sharp knife (or the electric) slice it as you would a salami.

Fish are far easier to butcher if they're well chilled. The closer the flesh is to freezing, the firmer it is and the cleaner your cuts will be. I like to place the fish in a freezer for a few minutes prior to butchering. Be careful that the fish doesn't actually freeze; you only want to firm it for cutting. This process is called super-chilling, and is common practice in commercial fish processing plants.

Fish taste best when cooked fresh. If you want to freeze the fish for future consumption, dry it off with some paper towels, then wrap it in a Ziploc-style freezer bag, being careful to get all the air out. Wrap this package in aluminum foil, then place the foil pack in yet another freezer bag. Packed so, the fish will retain its freshness and flavor for up to four months. If you eat a lot of fish, invest in a small vacuum sealer. These wonderful devices aren't cheap, but are equally useful for chicken, beef, pork, and vegetables.

Although I do release the majority of the fish I catch, I have to admit that with a nice bottle of wine, or a couple of frosty beers, there isn't anything much more enjoyable than a delicious fish dinner. It's even better when the main course features a fish you've caught yourself. Taking care of your catch right from the start will ensure your meal is as fresh and tasty as possible.

CHAPTER 12

The Next Step

As I've said throughout this book, the joy of fishing is that you can keep it as simple, or make it as complex, as your heart desires. Chances are, though, that you'll find fishing raises more questions than it provides answers. If you're not catching anything, you can't help but wonder why. And if you are catching something, sometimes you wonder why, too: why are they in this particular spot at this time of day, eating these kinds of lures and baits? One of the truths of fishing is that the more you learn about it, the more you realize how little you know.

We're very fortunate to live in the time we do, for information on fishing has never been easier to obtain. For anglers who want to sharpen their skills, the answers are readily available. When I meet anglers who want to learn more about fishing, I suggest they do four simple things. The first of these is to read everything under the sun. Buy fishing books and subscribe to fishing magazines. You can't help but pick up a tip or two, whether it's general fishing information or specifics relating to tackle, presentation, or location. The more you know, the more effectively you can fish and thus make the most of your time on the water. All the best anglers I've met were fanatical readers, most with extensive libraries.

I'd also suggest watching television fishing shows. Although most of these programs place the emphasis on entertainment and rely on the host's personality or celebrity guests to carry the show, you can't help but learn a few things by watching them. Besides, what could be better entertainment than a fishing show on the big screen, backed by hi-fi stereo surround sound? Pass the chips!

If you're really serious about learning more, invest in your pastime by every now and then hiring a top fishing guide for a day. Spending time on the water with a professional guide is without doubt one of the very

best ways to shorten the learning curve. Be upfront before you book; tell the guide precisely what it is you want to learn. Although a day with one of these pros will set you back a couple of hundred bucks, there's simply no better way to master a new technique, learn to use a particular type of tackle, or find out how to catch fish in certain types of conditions.

Some professional tournament organizations offer what are called pro-am tournaments, which is short for professional-amateur. These events pair top professional anglers with amateur partners, most often through a random draw held each day of the event. The pros compete against the other pros, while the amateurs compete against the other amateurs. It can cost anywhere from $100 to $500 or more for an amateur angler to enter one of these events. Although participating in the tournament does give you the opportunity to win some pretty impressive prize money, the real benefit is that for a relatively low fee you get to spend two or three days on the water with some of the best anglers on the continent. And because they're fishing for big prize money and their reputations are at stake, they pull out all the stops. If you've ever wondered what it would be like to spend a day in the boat with top anglers like Denny Brauer, Roland Martin, Rick Clunn, or Bob Izumi, here's your chance. You'll learn more inside tricks and secret techniques than you ever imagined. And you might just get lucky and walk away with a new truck or boat.

Finally, to really learn about fishing, *go fishing!* Spend as much time on the water as you can. Going fishing when the conditions are terrific allows you to experiment, trying new spots and techniques with incredible confidence. If you know the fish are on and you can depend on getting a lot of bites, you can try things you wouldn't normally do. Sometimes you stumble across a location or a new technique that yields surprising results, and then you file it away in your mental notebook. If you're catching fish on every cast by slowly retrieving a big Mepps spinner just above the weeds, you may wish to experiment with a different lure or a different technique. Every now and then you'll find something that works even better. Again, you file that information away, saving it for a day when the standard approaches aren't producing much action.

It's just as valuable to go fishing when conditions positively stink. Most veteran anglers agree that one of the most difficult things to do in freshwater fishing is consistently catch walleye after a cold front. So that's precisely when I *want* to go walleye fishing, since there's no better time to experiment and learn how to catch these fish than when they're not in the mood. I already know I can catch them when conditions are ideal. For me, the challenge lies in learning how to catch them when the weather isn't so good.

Joining a local fishing club is a wonderful way to learn about fishing in your area, and make some great friends besides. It also gives you an opportunity to put something back. Most people find that simply spending time outdoors with a fishing rod in hand stirs the naturalist within them. The places where fish are found tend to be beautiful, so it's quite natural to become somewhat protective of the fish and their environment. Thus a great many fishing clubs exist not only for the social opportunities but also to manage grassroots-level habitat enhancement initiatives. Whether it's operating a little jar hatchery to stock more fish, trucking in gravel to create reefs and spawning habitat, planting trees to stabilize shorelines and create shade to lower water temperatures, or participating in stock assessment studies, fishing clubs across North America have been rolling up their collective sleeves and putting money and volunteer labor into conservation efforts for decades. Many anglers find that by directly participating in these initiatives, they close the loop and truly become one with their pastime. And philanthropy aside, the snacks served at these deals are usually pretty good.

Fishing is what you make it. For most of us it becomes a lifelong obsession. I still laugh when I think of some of the excuses I've come up with in order to sneak away from work and go fishing. There's just something about turning company time into time on the water that's incredibly sweet. Those stolen days are always the best ones. For years I had a nagging back problem that necessitated frequent visits to one mysterious Dr. Pike. Although the good doctor never did manage to cure my achy back, those afternoon appointments kept my freezer filled with chunky fillets and my photo album stuffed with happy memories.

When I changed jobs and went to work for a fishing magazine, it became tougher to sneak away, since my boss clearly suspected that my requested time off to attend a funeral had something to do with the impending opening of walleye season. An acquaintance named Gord occasionally phoned in complaining of a strange fever that necessitated his spending the day in bed. Only other anglers knew that his fevers involved muskie, and that "bed" was actually the name of his boat.

Did I mention this fishing thing can become addictive? Too late now. Enjoy!

Glossary

Adipose fin
Small, fleshy fin without rays found on the back of some fish, including trout, salmon, and catfish.

Anal fin
Rayed fin located on the lower body near the anus.

Anti-reverse
Mechanism in fishing reels that prevents the reel from rotating in reverse gear, creating a huge tangle of line.

Artificial
Short for artificial lure, as opposed to a natural bait.

Automatic reel
Battery-powered, motorized fishing reel designed for use by handicapped anglers.

Backing
Strong line used in fly fishing as a backup for the fly line. If a fish runs off a long distance, peeling all the flyline from the reel, it is said to go "into the backing."

Backlash
Tangle incurred while casting, usually caused by failure to thumb a baitcasting reel or too much line on a spinning reel. Also known as a "professional overrun."

Backtrolling
Trolling with the boat in reverse gear, proceeding stern-first. Backtrolling can provide greater control in presenting lures, and allows you to go slower than you can in forward gear.

Bail
Wire arm on the front of a spinning reel, used to pick up the line at the end of a cast and help feed it back onto the spool during the retrieve.

Bait

In the strictest term, a natural, organic food used to catch fish, including minnows, worms, crayfish, leeches, frogs, and grasshoppers. The term is sometimes used to describe any offering presented to the fish, natural or synthetic.

Baitcasting reel

Type of fishing reel that uses an exposed, rotating spool mounted perpendicular to the rod.

Barb

Sharp projection immediately behind the point of a hook, used to keep the hook from sliding out of the fish in the course of the fight. Barbs may also be found farther up the hook shank, where they are used to hold bait in place.

Blank

Main component, or shaft, in a fishing rod.

Bobber

Slang term for a float, normally used in reference to inexpensive models.

Bottom bouncer

Sinker designed for use when trolling, consisting of a heavy cylindrical weight located midway along a wire shaft.

Bucktail

Deer hair, most often used in making flies or as a dressing on jigs and muskie lures.

Buzzbait

Surface lure consisting of a wire shaft, a metal blade, and a single hook.

Carolina rig

Another name for a slip sinker rig, involving a slip sinker, a swivel, a length of monofilament line, and a hook.

Catfish

Family that includes several species of popular freshwater game fish, easily identifiable by their whisker-like barbels around the mouth.

Caudal fin

Proper name for the fish's tail fin.

Chart

Short for "navigational chart," which offers a three-dimensional representation of the bottom of navigable lakes and rivers. Helpful for finding fishing spots.

Crankbait

Collective term for several varieties of artificial lures that generate a wriggling action when pulled through the water. (The name refers to cranking the reel to make them work.)

Crayfish

Popular live bait for largemouth bass, smallmouth bass, and walleye.

Dorsal fin

Fins located on the fish's back (dorsal) surface.

Downrigger

Manual or electric winch with a heavy weight, attached to a boat, used to take fishing lures to a pre-determined depth when trolling. A release mechanism frees the line from the weight when a fish hits, allowing it to be played in the conventional manner.

Drag

Slipping clutch mechanism in fishing reels that allows the reel to surrender line under stress, preventing the line from breaking.

Drop-off

Term commonly used to describe areas in lakes and rivers where a rapid depth change occurs.

Dry fly

Artificial fly intended to be used on the water's surface.

Eutrophic

Term used to describe lakes and rivers with high nutrient levels.

Fish finder

Consumer version of sonar, used by anglers in boats to determine depth, to find structures like shoals and reefs that should attract fish, and occasionally to spot fish themselves.

Flat

Expansive flat spot on a lake or river bottom. With weed growth, flats can be fish magnets.

Float

Device used to suspend a bait or lure in the water, which may be fixed in place on the line or allowed to slide freely.

Gaff

Large barbless hook on a handle, used to land fish.

Grub

Generic name for small, soft plastic worms with thin, flat, C-shaped tails that wriggle when pulled through the water.

Guides

Metal or synthetic rings on a fishing rod that the line passes through.

Hardware

Slang term for artificial lures, particularly metal lures such as spinners.

Jerkbait

Family of typically large, multi-hook lures for pike and muskie, given action by the angler by sharply jerking them through the water.

Jig

Family of artificial lures consisting of a weighted single hook dressed with feathers, hair, live bait or a soft plastic lure.

Leader

Length of wire at the end of a fishing line, used to prevent bite-offs by sharp-toothed fish such as pike and muskie. Leader can also refer to a length of line between the hook and another item of terminal tackle, such as a swivel or sinker.

In fly fishing, the term leader describes a length of tapered monofilament attached to the end of the fly line.

Mesotrophic
Term used to describe lakes and rivers of moderate nutrient levels.

Minnowbait
Long, slender crankbaits designed to mimic a small fish.

Monofilament
Most common type of fishing line, monofilament is created from a single, solid strand of extruded nylon.

Nightcrawler
Common variety of earthworm, normally from six to eight inches (15–20 cm) in length.

Oligotrophic
Term used to describe lakes and rivers with low nutrient levels.

Panfish
Collective term used to describe yellow perch, white bass, and various members of the sunfish family. Panfish are so named for their size—they nicely fit a frying pan.

Pectoral fin
Fin normally found on each side of the fish's body immediately behind the gill opening.

Pelvic fin
Pair of adjoining fins normally found midway along a fish's belly, sometimes immediately behind the gill openings, below the pectoral fins.

PFD
Personal flotation device; a life jacket or Floater coat.

Pitching
Technique of short-range underhand casting that allows the lure to enter the water with minimal disturbance.

Plug
Term once commonly used to describe wooden and plastic crankbaits.

Point
Area where vegetation, rock, or stone extends from the shoreline in an obvious finger-shaped mass. Great places to find fish.

Pole
Unlike rods, poles do not have guides for casting and are not used with a reel. Rather, a short length of line is simply tied to the end. Poles are well liked in some locations for their simplicity, and are used primarily for panfish.

Pool
Section of a river or stream characterized by greater depth and a slower current than surrounding areas. Pools provide fish with resting areas and protection from predators.

Pork
Preserved chunks of pork are popular artificial lures for some

species, particularly bass and pike. Pork chunks are often shaped to imitate frogs or leeches, and have a rippling action in the water.

Reef
Mass of rock or sand on the bottom of a lake, normally of less depth than the bottom surrounding it.

Reel seat
Section of a fishing rod handle to which the reel attaches.

Riffle
Shallow rapids in a creek or river.

Rise
Term used to describe the disturbance left by a fish, usually a trout, feeding on the surface.

Rod tube
Plastic or metal protective case for a fishing rod.

Roe
Salmon or trout eggs, commonly used as bait.

Run
Section of a river or stream characterized by a relatively flat bottom and steady current, not as fast or shallow as a rapids or riffle, yet not as deep and slow-moving as a pool. Runs are often used as feeding stations by fish. *Run* can also refer to seasonal migrations of fish, such as a salmon run.

Saddle
Area of shallow water in a lake, most often found between two or more islands, or between an island and the mainland.

Scent
Synthetic or natural compounds, usually liquid, applied to lures to increase their attraction to fish.

Shiner
One of several members of the minnow family, often sold as baitfish.

Sinker
Weight applied to a fishing line to take the lure or bait deeper.

Skirt
Dressing of silicone or soft rubbery fingers, used to adorn some types of lures, particularly buzzbaits and spinnerbaits.

Slab
Slang term for a particularly large panfish, usually a crappie.

Slip float
Float designed to slide freely on the line.

Slip sinker
Sinker designed to slide freely on the line.

Snag
Generally, a rock or log on the lake or river bottom that catches an angler's line. The term *snag* also refers to the act of hooking a fish by impaling it with the hook in the body rather than the mouth. Intentionally snagging fish is ille-

gal in most areas, and usually considered unethical.

Snap
Small wire clip that ties to the end of a fishing line and allows frequent lure changes without the need to continually tie knots.

Soft plastics
Large family of artificial lures designed to imitate worms, crayfish, insects, frogs, fish, and lizards, made from a soft plastic material and often impregnated with scents.

Spawn
See *Roe*.

Spincasting reel
Type of fishing reel that uses a fixed spool mounted parallel to the rod and encased within a plastic shroud or hood. Sometimes referred to as a closed-face reel.

Spinner
Type of artificial lure incorporating a flat metal or plastic blade that revolves quickly around a central wire shaft.

Spinnerbait
Type of artificial lure incorporating a weighted single hook fixed to a bent wire shaft, which holds a spinner blade above the hook, which is normally dressed with a soft plastic or silicone skirt.

Spinning reel
Type of fishing reel that uses an exposed, fixed spool mounted parallel to the rod. The most common type of reel, sometimes referred to as an open-face reel.

Split shot
Spherical lead sinker that attaches to a fishing line by inserting the line through a groove and pinching the sinker snugly into place.

Spoon
Type of artificial lure, made from metal or plastic, which resembles a spoon.

Still fishing
Fishing with live bait from a stationary position.

Stinger
Secondary hook sometimes attached to the end of an artificial lure to increase hooking percentage.

Stringer
Wire, chain, or rope used to tether fish intended for consumption.

Sucker
One of a large family of bottom-dwelling fish, easily identified by their underslung mouths.

Surface lure
Artificial lure designed to float at rest and mimic a frog or other creature moving along the surface of the water.

Suspender
Artificial lure that neither floats nor sinks at rest, but is designed to suspend itself in the water column.

Swivel
Small metal device designed to prevent twist in fishing lines.

Tailrace
Term used to describe the fast water below a dam or waterfall.

Terminal tackle
Collective term used to describe hooks, sinkers, snaps, leaders, and other accessories used primarily in live-bait fishing.

Texas rig
Method of rigging soft plastic lures in which the hook eye and point are imbedded in the lure to make it more resistant to fouling on submerged vegetation.

Tippet
A short section of thin monofilament line used between the leader and fly in fly fishing.

Topwater
Slang term used to describe fishing with surface lures.

Treble
Hook with three points, most often used on artificial lures.

Trolling
Presenting a bait or lure to fish by towing it behind a boat.

Tube
Cylindrical, soft plastic lure with a hollow body and fringed tail, somewhat resembling a small squid. Tubes are most often fished on a jig head.

Waders
Rubber, neoprene, or Gore-Tex boots that come up to the crotch or chest, used for fishing on foot in streams, rivers, and shallow bays.

Walleye
Largest member of the perch family.

Weedless hook
Specially designed hook that uses a wire or synthetic fiber to protect the point against fouling in vegetation.

Weedline
Typically, the edge of a weedbed; the distinct edge of an area of weed growth.

Wet fly
Fly designed to be fished beneath the water's surface.

Index